THE GOD OF FAITH AND REASON

The God of Faith and Reason

Foundations of Christian Theology

ROBERT SOKOLOWSKI

UNIVERSITY OF NOTRE DAME PRESS
NOTRE DAME   LONDON

Library of Congress Cataloging in Publication Data

Sokolowski, Robert.
     The God of faith and reason.

     Includes bibliographical references and index.
     1. Christianity — Philosophy.   2. Theology.
3. Faith and reason.   I. Title
BR100.S57   230'.2   81-19813
ISBN 0-268-01006-4   AACR2

Manufactured in the United States of America

TO FRANCIS SLADE

Nam in quem locum quisque ceciderit, ibi debet incumbere, ut surgat. For on whatever place one has fallen, on that place he must find support that he may rise again.

— St. Augustine,
De vera religione, XXIV, 45.

Contents

Preface

Christian faith is said to be in accordance with reason and yet to go beyond reason. This claim immediately gives rise to a difficulty. On the one hand the concordance of faith with reason seems to reduce Christian belief to rational thinking and to natural human experience; on the other hand the difference between faith and reason seems to make belief unreasonable and arbitrary.

The difficulty — like all theological difficulties — is not merely speculative. It has repercussions in Christian moral behavior, in education, and in the understanding Christians will have of their place in the world and in their social order. It will affect how the scriptures, prayer, the sacraments, and the church are understood, and will provoke the questions whether Christianity differs from other religions and whether Christian faith differs from natural religious experience.

This book treats the difficulty, not by speaking directly about faith and reason, but by examining the Christian understanding of God. The emphasis is, not on belief and reasoning, but on that which is believed and reasoned about. Our attention is turned toward God as creator and the world as created. The way creation is understood in Christian faith makes the Christian understanding of the divine different from the religious understanding achieved in natural experience and in other religious traditions. The Christian God is different from other gods; because of this, Christianity can preserve both the integrity of reason and the distinctiveness of faith.

Moreover the Christian sense of God as creator was most

completely disclosed in the life of Jesus and in the church's understanding of who and what Christ was. The New Testament and the teaching of the church do not only tell us about Christ; they also tell us about God. They tell us what God must be if Christ is to have been both human and divine. The Christian understanding of God as creator is thus related to Christian belief in Jesus and in the salvation he accomplished.

This book begins with a statement of the Christian understanding of God. This statement, in chapter one, is developed in terms provided by St. Anselm, in whose writings the issue of faith and reason surfaces in a historically significant way. Then, to bring out the special character of the Christian understanding of God, chapter two describes the pagan understanding of the divine, the foil against which Christianity first defined itself.

In chapter three the Christian understanding of God is related to a special way of distinguishing between God and the world. Chapter four shows how the Christian distinction between God and the world is different from distinctions made within the world (which is the normal setting for the exercise of reason). It also shows how the distinction was implied by the early Christological councils of the church. The distinction is shown to rest at the intersection of faith and reason. In chapter five the metaphysics of St. Thomas is interpreted as a development of the Christian distinction between God and the world, and mention is made of the need to keep the Christian doctrine of creation distinct from some Platonic and some contemporary philosophical themes that may seem to coincide with it.

Chapters six and seven deal with action, morals, and virtue and vice. In order to provide a setting for theological virtue, it is necessary to work out a more adequate understanding of natural virtue and vice than is currently available. This is done in chapter six, which is a study of Aristotle's ethical teaching. This chapter is not presented merely as a commentary on Aristotle; it is presented as a true account of human ethical behavior, one that avoids some serious obfuscations present in the way action and morals have been philosophically described in recent years. These ethical clarifications allow us to show, in chapter seven, how theological virtue differs from natural virtue and hence how moral theology differs from ethics. We also discuss what "action" might mean in the context provided by Christian belief and why grace is needed as a principle of such action. The chapter closes with some problems that arise when natural virtue is placed within the Christian setting and contrasted with the theological and infused virtues.

The problem of reconciling natural and theological virtue leads us to chapter eight, which also picks up the theme of the Christian distinction that had been developed in chapters three to five. In chapter eight we examine how the Christian distinction becomes manifest to us, how the Christian God is distinguished from the world and its necessities. The reflective study of how the Christian distinction between God and the world is presented to us is called the theology of disclosure. It is a dimension of theology that comes to terms with modern philosophical treatments of appearances or phenomena and with the historical emphasis found in modern thinking. But it comes to terms with them while preserving the classical Christian understanding of God and the world.

Chapter nine turns back to St. Anslem and shows how the Christian understanding of God is related to Anselm's argument that God exists. The difference between an argument and an understanding is explored, and the place of Christian action in establishing Christian understanding is discussed. Chapter ten turns to the scriptures. It tries to show how the Christian understanding of God and of Christ occurs in the New Testament texts and how it is related to the understanding of God found in the Old Testament. Chapter eleven asks in what sense there is an experience of the divine, as the divine is understood by Christian belief, and mentions the place of the teaching church in maintaining faith in the hidden God.

Finally, chapter twelve discusses the sacramental life, the life appropriate to Christian belief. In the sacraments the substantial presence and the actions of God take place, but the sacraments are also, essentially, signs; they reflect therefore the way God is understood in Christian belief, as the creator and redeemer who is always with us, but with us through faith.

There are three appendices to the book. The first two, dealing with Aristotle's concept of virtue and with Thomistic metaphysics, collect some technical materials germane to chapters six and nine. The third appendix deals with an important issue that has been underdeveloped in Christian theology, the relationship between political philosophy and Christian revelation. The writings of Leo Strauss are used to raise questions about political philosophy and faith, and the Christian distinction is used in replying to these questions. This section of the book is not simply a discussion of Strauss' ideas but an attempt to speak about the place of politics and political reason in Christian belief.

Some of the material in this book has been developed from a course I have given for several years to students beginning their program in theology. Many passages in the book were first formulated in response to questions and concerns raised by students in the course. The main purpose of the book is to make the philosophical and theological clarifications that are necessary to show that Christian mysteries, such as those involved in the doctrines of the Trinity, redemption, grace, the sacraments, and the church, can be stated as meaningful and true, that they can be asserted as real on their own terms, that they do not need to be deciphered into a merely symbolic or a simply human meaning. Theoretical clarifications do not, of course, substitute for faith or Christian action, but they do serve to open the logical space within which Christian mysteries can be acknowledged as mysteries. The Christian doctrine of creation and the Christian distinction between God and the world are the place where such clarifications are to be made.

I wish to thank Francis Slade and Thomas Prufer, who have helped me become aware of the issues that are central to this book. I am grateful to friends and colleagues whose thoughts may be reflected in this volume, especially Paulinus Bellet, O.S.B., and Owen Sadlier, O.S.F. My thanks are also due to Jude Dougherty, Joseph Zalotay, and Avery Dulles, S.J., for reading the manuscript and helping me with their comments.

1. Beginning with St. Anselm

In the Christian faith we are told about ourselves, about our history, and about the world. We are told both how things are and how they ought to be. But these teachings are coherent only when they are taken within a setting provided by a special understanding of God. Words like "incarnation" and "redemption," "eucharist," "charity," "sin," "conversion," and "hope," when used in a specifically Christian way, do not simply name things that show up in human experience; what they name is determined by the God who is involved with such things. God himself, as God, does not appear in the world or in human experience. He is not the kind of being that can be present as a thing in the world. And yet, despite this necessary absence, he is believed to be that which gives the definitive sense to everything that does appear in the world and in experience.

We first learn about the Christian God in the course of Christian living. We hear about him through preaching, we address him in prayer, and we attempt to respond to him in our actions; however, we approach him as one who will always be absent to us while we remain in something we now must call "our present state." But besides responding to God in prayer and in action, we can also attempt to think about him and about the relationship of the world to him; when such thinking discloses necessary elements and structures, it is called Christian theology. The primary task of Christian theology is to clarify how the God we believe in is to be understood. He is not a part of the world, and yet the world has its being and definitive sense from him. What kind of existence does he

I

enjoy and, consequently, what kind of being does the world enjoy in relation to him? Only when this issue is sufficiently clarified can we approach other things — like the history of salvation, the sacraments, Christian virtues, and the Christian moral life — in our theological reflection.

The sense of God as necessarily hidden and yet somehow pervasive in the world is expressed by St. Anselm of Canterbury. In the first chapter of his *Proslogion* he writes, *"Domine, si hic non es, ubi te quaeram absentem? Si autem ubique es, cur non video praesentem?* Lord, if you are not here, where shall I seek you, being absent? But if you are everywhere, why do I not see you present?"[1] The meaning of the adverbs — *hic, ubi, ubique* — and the meaning of *absentem* and *praesentem* in these sentences are to be determined by the argument of the rest of the work; the adverbs are not simply spatial terms but have a transformed theological sense, and the presence and absence are not the kind we are accustomed to when we look for a lost object, try to remember a name, or anticipate visiting a city we have never seen. Even the "here" in which God is not, is not simply the here of ordinary location. The sense of these theological places, presences, and absences will be determined by the sense of God established in chapter two of the *Proslogion*, which is entitled *"Quod vere sit Deus;* That truly God exists."

But still in chapter one Anselm expands the use of spatial expressions and joins them to terms which express the need to go "somewhere else" to find the God that he desires: *"ubi, quomodo accedam, quis me ducet, longinquus exsul, longe projectus, nimis abest illi facies tua, inaccessibilis est habitatio tua, nescit locum tuum;* where, how shall I come near, who will lead me, this faraway exile, cast far away, your face is very far from him, your dwelling is inaccessible, he does not know your place." This medley of places and spatial motions is accented by terms expressing vision and "face," the object of vision: *"ut videam te, numquam te vidi, anhelat videre te, ignorat vultum tuum, qua facie te quaeram, ad te videndum factus sum;* that I might see you, never have I seen you, he sighs to see you, he does not know your visage, under what aspect shall I seek you, to see you was I made." Because sight is a sense that covers spatial distances, the image of vision reinforces the spatial terms of location and motion in this paragraph.

In the next paragraph, the third in chapter one, terms signifying time are introduced as Anselm describes an earlier condition in which man enjoyed the presence of God, only to lose it and leave us all without it: *"o durus et dirus casus ille; misera mutatio; grave damnum, gravis dolor, grave totum*; o hard and cruel that fall; wretched change; grievous loss, grievous sorrow, grievous utterly." Anselm contrasts "then" and "now" and *ille* and *nos,* and while adding these temporal elements, he continues the earlier theme of spatial distances and motions to express the separation we suffer from the divine presence: *"unde sumus expulsi, quo sumus impulsi; unde praecipitati, quo obruti;* whence are we expelled, whither are we driven; whence cast down, whither submerged."

These expressions of separation and motion and place clearly involve metaphor. The original spatial sense of these words has been theologically transformed. However, spatial terms are metaphorically transformed to express many other things that are not theological. When we are said to turn our minds "toward" this issue, or to derive this conclusion "from" those premises, or to think this "about" that, we use spatial terms that have been adapted to speech about thinking and the objects of thought. What other kind of transformation is necessary to make the spatial terms serve theologically? How do we go "from" and "toward," how do we "approach" the presence of God?

It is true that the metaphorical use of such terms helps us realize that we are dealing with a special use of language, a special kind of motion and desire, and a special sense of the presence we hope to achieve and the absence we lament. We say there is motion "from" and "toward," but we insist it is not like spatial motion to and from something, and also not like the intellectual "motions" to and from something we think about when we do science and philosophy. We claim to be dealing with another kind of activity, and by insisting that the terms are to be taken metaphorically, we turn our minds and the minds of our listeners to the new dimension we wish to speak about.

The metaphors help disclose the new dimension; they do not merely ratify it. The disclosive function of metaphors helps engender and sustain our appreciation of God in the course of Christian life and faith. However, when we attempt to reflect theologically on Christian faith and experience, we do not simply add more metaphors to our religious discourse, nor do we simply repeat the metaphors we have been using. It becomes incumbent on us to disclose the space within which the metaphors move. We have to show why metaphors are necessary and what it is that they disclose. We have to speak directly about the dimension that is added to our ordinary, worldly experience, the dimension that calls for metaphorical transformations of our mundane language. This is not to say that theological reflection has a new kind of access to the objects of Christian religious discourse; the initial, ineluctable, and unsurpassable access to them is in Christian faith, but theology can disclose what it is in the object of Christian faith that demands a transformation of the language we use to talk about things in the world. St. Anselm carries out such a theological enterprise when he discusses the existence of God.

When Anselm begins to think about the God in whom he believes, the first issue that arises is the issue of unbelief. He describes the God of faith as being *"aliquid quo nihil maius cogitari possit*; something than which nothing greater can be thought."* Then in the very next sentence he asks, *"An ergo non est aliqua talis natura*; but perhaps there does not exist any such nature,"* and quoting Psalm 13, he mentions the *insipiens*, the fool, as a kind of authority for this position, an authority nested within the authority of scripture itself: the fool is cited as asserting that there is no God. This quick turn to unbelief as an issue is not simply an apologetical maneuver; it is required by the nature of rational inquiry. When we think about something and attempt to define and understand it, we do so by appreciating the object in contrast to its proper other, in contrast to what it specifically is not. We understand life when we are able to recognize and explain the nonliving as such; we understand and begin to define health when we can contrast it to disease. Making distinctions is the first step in the exercise of reason.

True, we may be acquainted with something without having contrasted it to its opposite and its negation, but we do not begin to understand unless such an exercise in contrasts takes place. Reason is the power of affirming and denying, and the possibility of affirmation and denial is based on our appreciation of things as contrasted to what they are not. When we wish to think theologically about faith, therefore, we must contrast faith to unbelief; and when we wish to think theologically about God as the object of faith, we must raise the question of the negation of "any such nature" as the God in whom we believe. Anselm will go on to show that the nonexistence of God is not thinkable, but the issue of his existence or nonexistence has to be raised before this theological conclusion is drawn.

Of course unbelief is encountered before we begin to think theologically, but then it is encountered as something to be overcome or resisted, not as an issue for theorizing. In the life of religious faith unbelief is taken as something the believer must avoid, just as disease and injuries are to be avoided in our bodily life. The Christian religious life is lived within faith, and the lack of faith is not included as an acceptable possibility inside that life. But when we attempt to think theologically about faith and its object, unbelief has to be included dispassionately as the proper foil and negative to the faith we wish to think about. Because of the contrastive nature of reason we cannot think theologically about faith and God without raising the issue of unbelief and the nonexistence of God. It might therefore seem to the believer that theological thinking threatens faith because it forces one to entertain the possibility of unbelief, and perhaps it was to dispel this aura of skepticism and incredulity that Anselm quoted someone mentioned in the scriptures themselves when he raised the issue of unbelief. But Anselm also goes on to show that the nonexistence of God is not thinkable, and he thereby demonstrates that faith has nothing to fear from rational inquiry. The God of Christian faith is such that reason cannot deny his existence. By establishing this security of faith before reason, Anselm opens the door to the reasoned exploration of faith that took place in scholastic theology; he lets loose the distinctions and principles that permitted the emergence of universities as institutions specific to the Christian world; and he provides the setting of the divine and the desirable within which reason has exercised itself during the thousand years now drawing to a close.

Anselm begins something new. Before him reason was used within faith, but it was not turned toward faith. In the earlier councils and in the work of the church fathers believers made distinctions, drew relationships and analogies, made identifications, defined things, settled arguments, and provided explanations; such activities were carried on within faith and they articulated what was believed. But in Anselm there is an attempt of reason to make belief itself its theme; the attempt is carried out by the serious entertainment of what the unbeliever might mean when he expresses the opposite of belief. And Anselm thinks about belief and unbelief, not in regard to some particular of the Creed, but in regard to the being of God. Reason seems here to establish a distance toward faith; it seems, in contrast to what it had done in previous centuries, to come out with a kind of independence, almost a claim to judgment over faith, even as Anselm continues to say that he does not try to understand in order to believe but believes in order to understand. The resolution of this emergence of reason is the insight that what was believed is maintained, not destroyed, when it is made a topic for thinking. Perhaps some of the happiness and relief Anselm says he experienced when he found his "single argument" comes from his appreciation that reason and Christian faith can both be themselves without threatening one another: "ut studiose cogitationem amplecterer; so that I eagerly embraced the thought; aestimans igitur quod me gaudebam invenisse, si scriptum esset, alicui legenti placiturum; judging then that what I rejoiced to have found would, if put in writing, give pleasure to anyone who might read it" (preface). But having found itself in this new context and having distinguished itself from faith, reason never returns to the simple assimilation in which it spent its earlier years of living with Christian belief. Anselm's discovery that faith is not threatened by reason is not only a reassurance for belief but a recognition that reason can act freely and publicly, on its own terms, within Christian faith.

Anselm may secure faith before reason, but does he not claim to do more than that? Does he not attempt to establish the existence of God apart from belief in him? He says in his preface that he wishes to discover "*unum argumentum, quod nullo alio ad se probandum quam se solo indigeret, et solum ad astruendum quod deus vere est . . . sufficeret*; a single argument which would require no other for its proof than itself alone, and alone would suffice to demonstrate that God truly exists." If this single argument requires nothing besides itself for its proof, does it not by itself establish the truth of the existence of God, and is it not independent of faith? This single argument is also supposed to establish "*quia est summum bonum nullo alio indigens, et quo omnia indigent ut sint et ut bene sint*; that there is a supreme good requiring nothing else, which all things require for their being and their well-being." And even more thoroughly, the argument is to demonstrate "*et quaecumque de divina credimus substantia*; and whatever we believe regarding the divine substance." If an argument can achieve all this, what is there left to believe? Anselm often asserts that one must believe in order to understand, but the argument he provides seems to stand on its own without the support of faith.

All commentators on Anselm admit that his argument takes place within a religious setting, but many insist that, however admirable the religious context, and however edifying the prayers that begin, accompany, and conclude his composition, the argument itself can be detached from its setting in faith and accepted or rejected entirely on its own. The simple thought of "that than which nothing greater can be thought" is all that is needed, and an argument can be built upon this thought, no matter where, when, or to whom it is presented. Anyone, even the *insipiens*, can understand this thought when he hears it expressed, and therefore the thought exists in his mind when he understands it.

The argument Anselm proposes in chapter two to show "that truly God exists" is based on the difference between existing in the mind, *in solo intellectu*, and existing in reality, *in re*. Anselm acknowledges this difference and says that it is greater, *maius*, to exist both in reality and in the mind than it is to exist merely in the mind. Then he draws his conclusion, that

God must be thought to exist; for if he were seen to exist only in the mind, he would not be appreciated as that than which nothing greater can be thought.

Anselm's argument works explicitly with the contrast between being in the mind and being in reality. This contrast, and the two ways of being that it distinguishes, are themselves deserving of further thought. But besides this explicit premise for his argument, there is another, an implicit premise, which the argument requires but which is not expressed openly by Anselm in chapter two. This implicit premise also contains a contrast. It might be formulated as the statement that:

(God plus the world) is not greater than God alone; or:

(God plus any creature) is not greater than God alone.

This unstated premise also involves something's being greater than something else, but it does not move between mental and extramental existence. The premise implies that God is to be so understood, and the world or creatures are to be so understood, that nothing greater, *maius*, is achieved if the world or creatures are added to God. To bring out this implication, and to state the premise in terms more akin to Anselm's own expression, we must say:

(God plus the world) cannot be conceived as greater than God alone; or:

(God plus any creature) cannot be conceived as greater than God alone.

Earlier in the *Proslogion*, in the preface, Anselm had stated this understanding of God when he said he wished to establish that God is the highest good "*nullo alio indigens*; requiring nothing else." This is the understanding of God that is needed for Anselm's argument; it is implied but not explicitly stated in the phrase "that than which nothing greater can be thought," for if the world or any creature were to contribute greatness to God, then God would not be that than which nothing greater can be thought. God plus the creature or God plus the world would be thinkable as greater than God alone. Anselm's definition of how God is to be understood is usually taken to mean that no other being, or no other combination of beings, could be conceived as greater than God; but it must also be true that any being or any beings taken together with God cannot be conceived as amounting to something greater than God alone. Anselm's formula does not just compare beings externally with God, after telling us how we are to think about God. The formula is more compressed and more inclusive; it contains a statement about how beings are to be understood, as well as a statement about how the relationship between beings and God is to be understood.

Furthermore, in chapters three and five Anselm introduces the theme of being better, *melius*, as parallel to the theme of being greater, so another formulation of his unstated premise would be:

(God plus the world) cannot be conceived as better than God alone; or:

(God plus any creature) cannot be conceived as better than God alone.

That is, no perfection would be lost if God had not created the world. The world and God must be so understood that nothing but God could be all that there is, and there would be no diminution of greatness or goodness or perfection. God is not better or greater because of creation, nor is "there" more goodness or greatness because God did create.[2] This does not imply that God does not care about his creation, or that what is created is not worth anything. On the contrary, God's benevolence is so great that even though he does not need creation in any sense at all — he does not need it to be himself, nor does he need it for "there" to be greater excellence; *nullo alio indigens* — still he has created and, beyond that, has entered into his creation in the person of Jesus.

This is how God is to be understood in Anselm's writing, and this is how beings are to be understood in relation to God.

Before examining this understanding of God, and before showing how it is necessary for Anselm's argument, we might observe what it has to tell us about the setting within which
Anselm reasons. This understanding of God, as capable of being
without the world, as capable of being all that there is, with no
lessening of goodness or greatness, is a Christian understanding.
It is not the appreciation that pagans have of the divine, and it
is not that which naturally comes to mind when people think
about the sacred and the ultimate. If this understanding of God
is necessary for Anselm's argument, then the Christian
influence does not extend only to the prayers and the motives
that surround the argument; it enters into the definition of the
terms that support Anselm's reasoning. Anselm's argument
could not be detached from the Christian setting in which it
occurs, because the understanding of God that it implies has
arisen and is sustained in Christian faith. And yet, nevertheless,
there is something simply "reasonable" about Anselm's argument and about his understanding of God. This is why Anselm
is so strategic a figure in the differentiation of reason and faith,
and why the issue of how they are related each to the other is
appropriately explored through a reading of his texts. The explicit moves in Anselm's argument, which have drawn sufficient
attention to themselves, are less interesting, theologically and
philosophically, than the implied understandings, of God and of
reason, that permit the moves he makes.[3]

NOTES

1. St. Anselm's Proslogion, translated with introduction and commentary by M.J. Charlesworth (1965; reprinted., Notre Dame: University
of Notre Dame Press, 1979). This book gives both the Latin and the
English. For the English in my text I have used Charlesworth's translation and that by S.N. Deane in St. Anselm: Basic Writings (La Salle:
Open Court, 1962), but have made adaptations and changes.

2. Later, in chapter 20, Anselm reinforces this by invoking the
possibility of creatures' ceasing to exist: "You are in no way less,
even if they should return to nothing."

3. I am indebted to Thomas Prufer for his thoughts and formulations concerning the Christian theological sense of God, creation, and the world. See his essay "Notes for A Reading of Augustine, *Confessions*, Book X, *omni secreto interior, omni honore sublimior*" to appear in *Interpretation*.

2. Pagan Divinity

The issue of creation has been discussed by theologians and philosophers for so long that the unusual character of the question has become forgotten. It seems to be obvious that men should observe the contingency of the world and ask themselves why there is something rather than nothing. But such issues do not arise automatically wherever there are men, even if the men are thoughtful. If we examine pagan thinking about the divine, we do not find the issue of creation raised in the way it is raised in Christianity, nor do we find the understanding of God that is maintained by Christians. In Greek and Roman religions, and in Greek and Roman philosophies, god or the gods are appreciated as the most powerful, most independent and self-sufficient, most unchanging beings in the world, but they are accepted within the context of being. Although god or the gods are conceived as the steadiest and most complete beings, the possibility that they could be even though everything that is not divine were not, is not a possibility that occurs to anyone. The being of pagan gods is to be a part, though the most important part, of what is; no matter how independent they are, the pagan gods must be with things that are not divine.

It is clear that the Olympian gods are understood as particular beings in the world. They are the expression of necessities that men encounter in the world, necessities that men must respect. Zeus, Poseidon, Ares and Aphrodite, the Muses, and Apollo are agents that rule over their particular domains, and they are the causes, the ones responsible, for what happens. Some of the gods rule over and in natural

phenomena; others, the gods of the city, are involved in political events; still others are related to families. As far as human
beings are concerned, the gods represent necessities that must
be accepted and against which a man can pretend to act only at
his peril. Men do not have a choice to go along with what has
to be; man's ability to recognize the gods is the ability to recognize and name necessities that will take their place, in him or
around him, whether he wants them to or not. Whether there
will be a storm or wind, whether war will come, whether he
will love this one or that, whether he will be angry, and
whether or not he will know what to say — all such things
occur to human beings; they are not, in this understanding of
the world, done by human beings. During the short time he
lives, a human being, one of the mortals, those that have to die,
is drawn off into these necessary motions and absorbed in
them, and yet he remains the while the one that he is. And
strangest of all, while these things have to be the way they are,
and while they go their own way, the man caught in them is
allowed to watch what happens and may see it all with a very
clear eye (as Homer, for one, was able to do); what happens is
not simply hidden from him. This sense of being caught in
necessity can even make someone think that things he does not
want to do, things that he deeply regrets or is ashamed to
perform, things that are criminal or outrageous, can come
about in him through the power of the gods; and all he can do
is bewail the tragic episode that was fated for him. He possesses the dismal independence of being aware of what is going
on, but of having no mastery over it.

Still, to recognize and to name the gods that have their way
with human beings does illuminate the human condition, and
the clarification it gives can be progressively developed. The
stories about the gods were not fixed in Greek tradition. The
poets were theologians who would reinterpret the myths and
formulate shifts of position and of relation among the gods and
the other mythical beings, to bring out new aspects of what had
to be, aspects that different circumstances or greater insight
permitted to come into view. Hesiod has new things to say
about Prometheus, for example, and Aeschylus has still other

things to say about him. Aeschylus has Prometheus admit that
he both brought fire to men (the means for techn*ē* and for
control over parts of the world) and that he also hid from men
the time and circumstances of their death. Prometheus made
the mortals unable to foresee the death measured out for them
and placed "blind hopes" in them (*Prometheus Bound*, 250– 52).
Because men henceforth did not know the day they were to die,
they were caught in a combination of certainty and ignorance:
they knew that they must die, but they did not know when or
how. This combination of assurance and blindness is necessary
to men as a spur to use fire, and all that fire allows, to hold off
death as long as possible. If men did not know they had to die,
or if they knew but also knew when and how they would die,
they would not in either case need to use their instruments and
their skills to extend human life. To know not just that human
beings are mortal, but that they are mortal in this strange mixture of knowledge and ignorance, and that their use of fire,
tools, and skills is conditioned by being mortal in this way, is to
know more about Prometheus, and it is to know it against the
necessities that had previously been registered in Hesiod and
the myths prior to him. The myths and the stories of the gods
are not what we would dismiss as fairy tales; they involve thinking about the necessities that condition human existence, the
terms under which human being is given and which we have no
choice but to accept. To become aware of these terms, even if
the awareness is formed as the fearful submission of men to
the gods (those reminders of what men prefer to forget), is
better than to think that there are no necessities in the world in
which we live.

When we now talk about this subjugation of human beings
to the gods, we speak of it as something long since dissipated.
The first distinction of human being from that which is ruled
by the Homeric gods took place in the Greek enlightenment.
Both the sophists and the presocratic philosophers accuse the
poets of projecting human characteristics on the gods; to make
such an accusation, the sophists and the philosophers must
have begun to appreciate human independence in a new way.
To see the gods as human projections is to see man as capable

of projecting the gods, and it breaks the spell they have over
him. It is to take man as more active in his involvement in the
world than he, in his animistic naivety, had given himself credit
for being. But although the gods began to fade from the many
necessities and events they had been thought to inhabit, neither
the sophists nor the philosophers denied the divine, nor did
they deny that there were necessities. The necessities became
simply the way things were born to be; they became that which
is "by nature," as opposed to that which is because of human
making or because of human choice. And the divine withdrew
to those forms of being that were taken to be the independent,
ruling substances in the world. The divine was part, the best
and governing part, of nature, but its direct involvement with
human affairs was no longer acknowledged nor was it feared.

In talking about the highest, celestial substances, for example, Aristotle says that the ancient myths told us "that these are
gods and that the divine encloses the whole of nature." He then
says that many human features were added to the gods in order
to pacify and guide the multitude, and he clearly rejects such
accretions. However, he says that the first point, "that they
thought the first substances to be gods," ought to be taken as
an "inspired (*theîos*) statement." He concludes by saying that
"to this extent only is the ancestral opinion, and that of our
first predecessors, clear to us" (*Metaphysics* XII 8, 1074b2 – 14).
That is, Aristotle finds in the myths something to be repeated
and maintained, provided the divine is withdrawn from the
lower substances we find in the world and placed in the highest
and first substances that govern the world. This divine part of
the world serves as the cause of motion and development in
other things; by a kind of final causation it draws other beings
to imitate, in their own appropriate ways, its permanence and
independence. The celestial bodies imitate it by their regular
circular motions, in which every departure is immediately the
beginning of a return to the place the body has left; and sublu-
nary substances imitate it by the continual reproduction that
keeps each species living on the earth. No matter how Aristotle's god is to be described, as the prime mover or as the self-
thinking thought, he is part of the world, and it is obviously

necessary that there be other things besides him, whether he is
aware of them or not. And the necessities that are left in our
world are to be explored and defined by philosophers, not only
by the theologian poets. Aristotle recognizes the necessities in
nature and even acknowledges man's subordination to them
when he observes that "the nature of men is enslaved in many
ways" (*Metaphysics* I 2, 982b29 – 30). But the necessities are to
be disclosed by reason as the way things simply have to be, not
described by poets as the way someone wants them to be.

While Aristotle sees the divine agencies withdrawn from
natural substances, he also sees man emerge as an agent that
has some power to determine himself and the world in which
he lives. Since Heraclitus (fragment 119), the Greeks had
known that men are led in life not by a daimon but by their
character or ethos, by the way they stabilize into acting, and
Aristotle shows how character is in turn shaped by the actions
we perform. He goes on to describe, in his ethical treatises, the
elements of human being that are involved in becoming an
agent and in making choices. Human agency in all its dimensions is recognized on its own terms and is not allowed to be
lost in the circumstances and natures that condition it. But
Aristotle realizes that human action is conditioned by many
necessities and limited in many ways. Men can think about
what they are capable of effecting, but they are also aware of
things they can do absolutely nothing about, things that are
simply the objects of an onlooker's *theōria*, not objects that men
can determine this way or that. Aristotle emphasizes that man
is not the best thing in the world, hence practical knowledge is
not the best knowledge: it is better to know the things that are
greater and more divine than man, the things that are especially
studied in first philosophy, the science that Aristotle sometimes
calls theological.[1] The theoretical exercise of reason is called
the most divine thing in man: "If reason is divine then, in
comparison with man, the life according to it is divine in comparison with human life" (*Nicomachean Ethics* X 7, 1177b30 – 31;
1177b26 – 1178a8). Aristotle thus considers the divine to be the
best part — but still only a part — of the cosmos; he sees
human being as independent of the mythical gods, but still
subordinated to necessities in many ways; he recognizes human

agency and its effects, but he also recognizes what is by nature as being there before men act, and as being there whether men act or not; and he sees man in some contact with the divine through the exercise of reason and in the attempt to know the first substances and first causes.

Plato's appreciation of being, the divine, and the human is not, in its fundamentals, very much different from what we have found in Aristotle. Coming before Aristotle and using a dramatic form of writing, Plato was in more immediate contact with the mythical understanding of things and pushed more directly against the myths in differentiating himself from them; he himself sometimes uses myths and constantly uses metaphors for positions that Aristotle would bring to literal expression. But there is the same acknowledgment of human agency, the same withdrawal of the gods from immediate control over nature and human affairs, and the same recognition of the divine as the best that there is, the motive and the object of the exercise of reason. In the *Symposium*, for example, all the varied Homeric gods become subordinated to Eros, the expression of desire (195C— 197E), but Eros himself becomes subordinated, in Socrates' speech, to the reasoned discrimination between what is right and wrong and true and false (198D— E); the life of thinking is more real in human affairs than is what happens *to* us.[2] But the life of reason itself, the striving to be truthful, is a religious endeavor which moves toward the divine (211A— 212A). As Socrates claims in the *Apology*, this life is undertaken not out of curiosity but in response to the god (20E— 21E) and in obedience to him (23A— B). Plato recognizes the divine as what Aristotle would call the first causes of things, even as he acknowledges human action as determined by what the human being wants and does. In the myth in the closing pages of the *Republic* Plato has Lachesis, one of the daughters of Necessity, speak through a herald to the "souls that live for a day" who are to choose among the lives presented to them. The souls are told that "a daimon will not select you, but you will choose a daimon," that "virtue is without a master," and that "the blame belongs to him who chooses; god is blameless" (617D— E). This may be a warning from Lachesis to the souls, but it is a proclamation from Plato to those who read his texts. Nevertheless, this enlightenment concerning human agency, this awareness that the most important thing is, not to placate something or someone, but to acquire "the capacity and the knowledge to distinguish the good and the bad life, and so everywhere and always to choose the better from among those that are possible" (618C), does not fail to recognize the divine as that which lets there be choice, knowledge, and human being, as well as the things that are in the world surrounding and surpassing man.

In Plato the divine does not take the substantial form of a prime mover or a self-thinking mind; it reaches its highest state in something beyond substance. But even the One or the Good is taken as "part" of what is: it is the One by being a one over, for, and in many, never by being One only alone by itself. Plato's notion of what is divine and ultimate is more elusive than the god of Aristotle; more elusive than the even more thing-like gods of the Epicureans, the eternal conglomerations of atoms, living their carefree lives in the spaces between the worlds; and more elusive than the Stoic divinity, the all-governing mind-stuff that pervades the world and guides it through the developments that are fated for it. But in all these cases, the divine, even in its most ultimate form, is never conceived as capable of being without the world. It is divine by being differentiated from what is not divine and by having an influence on what is not divine. The One of Plato is on the margin of, and in touch with, the many; it lets the many and the variegated be what they are. Even the One written about by Plotinus, which is placed still further "beyond" being than it is in Plato's writings, and which shows the influence of religious and speculative beliefs different from those of Greece, cannot "be" without there also being its reflections and its emanations in the other hypostases (the Mind and the Soul) and in the things of the world. The Plotinian One may not want or need anything else to be itself, so other things do not arise in order to make up any deficiency in the One; but such other things are still not understood as being there through a choice that might not have been made.

It is natural for human reason to find itself within the context of the world, to come up against the world and its necessities as simply there, as the extreme margin of what can be thought. To think or to believe beyond the setting of the world and its necessities should be recognized for the unusual movement that it is. It is not the case that the Greek philosophers were somehow not sufficiently intelligent, or that they did not strain their minds enough, to reach a distinction that reason should come to at some time or other. The step into understanding beings as possibly never having been at all is not like the step from Homer to Plato, from the mythical articulation of things into the literal and philosophical exploration of them. It is not simply one more pace in the march of reason, or one more refinement in human self-understanding. It is a movement of a very different kind.

In Christian belief we understand the world as that which might not have been, and correlatively we understand God as capable of existing, in undiminished goodness and greatness, even if the world had not been. We know there is a world, so we appreciate the world as in fact created, but we acknowledge that it is meaningful to say that God could have been all that there is. Such a "solitary" existence of God is counterfactual, but it is meaningful, whereas it would not be meaningful for the pagan sense of the divine. To use terms similar to those of Anselm, such an idea of God can exist in our minds; we can understand God in this way. Our understanding of God is that he would be "the same" in greatness and goodness whether he creates or does not create, and whether he creates or does not create depends only on his freedom. When God does create, there may be "more" but there is no "greater" or "better." And the world must be understood appropriately, as that which might not have been. The world and everything in it is appreciated as a gift brought about by a generosity that has no parallel in what we experience in the world. The existence of the world now prompts our gratitude, whereas the being of the world prompts our wonder.[3]

NOTES

1. See *Nicomachean Ethics* VI 7, 1141a20– 23, 1141a34– b2; *Metaphysics* VI 1, 1026a10– 19; XI 7, 1064a33– b3.

2. See Gerhard Krüger, *Einsicht und Leidenschaft: Das Wesen des platonischen Denkens*, 4th ed. (Frankfurt: Klostermann, 1973), pp. 95– 99, 134– 40. I have used, with slight changes, the translation by Allan Bloom for passages from the *Republic* (New York: Basic Books, 1968).

3. For some helpful remarks on the relationship between the pagan gods and Christianity see Christopher Derrick, "The Desacralization of Venus," *America*, September 12, 1981, pp. 106– 9.

3. Voices Expressing
the Christian Distinction

Theologically, the meaning of the divine as understood by Christians is best brought out when it is contrasted to the pagan sense of the world and the gods. To try to determine the conceptual boundaries of Christian belief by comparing it with contemporary atheism would give a skewed understanding of Christianity, because the denial of Christian belief is to some extent defined by Christian notions and permeated by them. The special differentiation that determines Christianity is brought out more originally in its contrast with pagan religion and philosophy.

In addition, it is especially important in Christian thinking to remain aware of the weight of natural necessities: the way things are and the way things have to be according to their various natures, whether material or biological, political or psychological, social or aesthetic; whether a picture or a pattern of exchange, the structure of time or of space, whether the essence of writing or of remembering. All things have their own natures and their excellence according to their kind. Now every form of understanding brings along its own special forms of concealment and misunderstanding; if one begins to think beyond the world and its necessities, instead of approaching them precisely as that beyond which there is nothing to think, the danger arises that one will simply deny the terminal and necessary character that is proper to them even within Christian belief. The move into the Christian understanding of the world must be so achieved that the integrity of natural necessities is maintained. But once a setting beyond the setting of the world is introduced, it becomes all too possible to treat the natural necessities in a frivolous way. Even in a pagan world, natural necessities may be treated frivolously by people who are not able to comprehend them, but a false sense of creation can seem to encourage and legitimate such undiscernment. Instead of allowing the light of creation to enhance what is natural and to confirm it in its goodness and necessity, the "light" may be used to make the natural and the necessary fade — in which case it serves not as light, which is supposed to make colors appear, but as a bleaching agent that makes them vanish. Thus a vivid appreciation of philosophical truth not only helps us see what is specifically new in Christian belief but also helps us preserve the integrity of nature within Christian faith.

Our ability to think theologically about creation is made more difficult by the tradition of modernity within which our thinking now has to take place. We do not simply stand before the contrast between paganism and Christianity, as the early Christians did; we are also confronted with the changes in the understanding of virtue and politics that have taken place since Machiavelli and Hobbes, and we must face the interpretation of science and nature that has developed since Bacon and Descartes. These and other currents in modernity are partly defined as rejections of both Christianity and antiquity, and many of the teachings we find in modernity could hardly be understood except as subsequent to Christian belief. In the opinions that are dominant and taken for granted in the Western world, nature is not seen as the pattern of necessities in man and the world; it is rather taken as that which is to be mastered and transformed by man. Nature is defined in function of technology and the human projects technology serves. Science, the highest activity of reason, is seen, not as the disclosure of the necessities in things and in the cosmos as a whole, but as the development of methods of calculation and control over nature. Man is seen less as a living thing embedded in a world, and more as a knower detached from the world that he tries to control.

When we say therefore that Christianity is best appreciated, theologically, by being contrasted with paganism, and that such a contrast helps to preserve the integrity of nature and reason, the modern overtones in words like "nature" and "reason" make it hard for us to bring out the theological and philosophical distinctions that we need. Moreover, because Christianity incorporates a sense of natural necessities within its understanding of the world as created, it is often put into conflict with the scientific enterprise that is so much a part of modernity; the tension between "science and religion" is largely the issue whether or not technology is to be restricted by anything like human nature or the natures of things. If religion were to renounce any claim to say anything about what is natural to people or to things, "science" would have little to quarrel with in it. Our attempt to clarify the sense of the natural and the divine will also serve consequently to emphasize the natural against post-Christian tendencies to obscure it.

Christian theology is differentiated from pagan religious and philosophical reflection primarily by the introduction of a new distinction, the distinction between the world understood as possibly not having existed and God understood as possibly being all that there is, with no diminution of goodness or greatness. It is not the case that God and the world are each separately understood in this new way, and only subsequently related to each other; they are determined in the distinction, not each apart from the other. The Christian distinction between the world and God may receive its precise verbal formulation in a theoretical context, since it is described especially by theologians and philosophers, but the distinction does not emerge for the first time in this theoretical setting. It receives its formulation in reflective thought because it has already been achieved in the life that goes on before reflective thinking occurs. The distinction is lived in Christian life, and most originally it was lived and expressed in the life of Jesus, after having been anticipated, and hence to some extent possessed, in the Old Testament history which Jesus completed. The Christian distinction between God and the world is there for us now, as something for us to live and as an issue for reflection, because it was brought forward in the life and teaching of Christ, and because that life and teaching continue to be available in the

life and teaching of the church. This is how the Christian understanding of God as creator, the understanding that Anselm
formulates for us, has been in fact achieved. In what sense such
an understanding could be achieved apart from the life of
Christian faith will be an issue for us later, but there is no
question of the fact, which is a massive fact theologically and
philosophically, that this understanding arose and is maintained
in Christian belief.

But even though the Christian distinction between God and
the world is first lived and then theoretically formulated, the
very living of the distinction involves words and teaching.
Christ did not only do things; he also taught and proclaimed
the kingdom of God. Such teaching and proclamation are not
theoretical reflection, but they do involve words and understanding. When we now try to live the Christian distinction
between God and the world, we too involve words and thoughts
in this life, even though words and thoughts without actions are
not enough for it. In fact, words and thoughts are necessary for
us even to know that this living of the Christian distinction
between God and the world is possible: "How are they to believe him of whom they have not heard? And how are they to
hear, if no one preaches? . . . Faith then depends on hearing,
and hearing on the word of Christ" (Romans 10:14,17). When it
was first proclaimed, the word of Christ was accompanied by
the actions of Christ, and when the word of Christ is repeated
by believers and by the church, it is to be accompanied by
actions in imitation of Christ; but it is also possible for the
word to rise above the inadequacies of those who express it,
and to bring about an intensity of life that could not be explained simply by the actions of those who hand it on.

The Christian distinction between God and the world needs
then to be stated as well as lived, and it can be stated only by a
voice. There are several voices that make the distinction available and insistent for us. There is the voice of scripture, particularly that of the New Testament, and there is the voice of
the church; behind and in both of these there is the voice of
Christ himself. There is in the church the voice of all the believers, those who live and express their faith in Christ, and

among the believers there is the special voice of the bishops and the pope. There is also the voice of the theologians, those who think reflectively about the faith and what is believed in it. All these voices are united and related to one another because they state the same thing; they are all established as voices because they express the Christian sense of God and the world. But they are distinguished as voices from one another because they express the same distinction, between God and the world, in different ways. How do they differ from each other?

The New Testament grew out of the early life of the church, and it was determined and closed as sacred scripture by the church; the church judged which writings were to be included in the Bible. The "creed" was prior to the scriptures. Furthermore, the scriptures are kept alive, are maintained as sacred, within the church. The church therefore contains the scriptures. However, the scriptures, and particularly the New Testament, are not merely a law or a treatise or a collection of maxims. The center of the New Testament is a narrative, and it presents not only the sayings but also the actions of Jesus. The Gospels tell us what happened and what was done in the life of Christ. When the church contains the New Testament, it contains a narrative that in turn presents the actions and events that make up the life of Jesus. The church is there to tell people what occurred in the life of Christ, and to make it possible for those occurrences to be repeated in the lives of those who believe in him. The life of the church is a history in which the events of the life of Jesus are not only commemorated and imitated but somehow repeated and made present again. Therefore in containing the scriptures, the church does not simply possess them as a part of itself: in the scriptures, in their narration, the church has presented not only its own origins but its substance. The voice of the church presents itself as a voice that repeats and echoes, and what it repeats and echoes was originally achieved in the words and events narrated by the Gospels. The church does not simply apply laws or interpret maxims, so its voice is not merely that of a judge, teacher, or legislator. It has to repeat and imitate things that happened, so its voice is necessarily involved with actions, actions which im-

itate, but also present again, the events narrated in the New
Testament writings.

The normal way in which the church repeats the words and
actions of Jesus is by proclaiming what he said and did and by
applying this message to present circumstances. This is done in
preaching, in the liturgy, in educating people in the Christian
life, and in the many ways the laity, religious, clergy, episco-
pate, and papacy express the faith. But because words and circumstances change, repetition sometimes involves controversy
as to what should be repeated. In such disagreements about the
truth of the Gospel the church engages the special teaching and
discriminating responsibility of the pope and bishops. It is part
of their office to determine whether or not a particular teaching
is identifiable or consistent with what is taught in the scriptures
and the tradition of the church. This special teaching function
is essentially the power to recognize sameness and difference
between what was taught and what is being proposed.[1] It is
part of Christian belief that when serious issues arise, the interpretation given by the church is authoritative, and that the
church so acting is preserved from errors that would make the
saving teaching of Christ no longer available to men. Very frequently positions that are judged to be heretical are those that,
by implication at least, blur the Christian distinction between
God and the world.

Because Christianity does not simply interpret the world and
the human condition, but proclaims a message presenting God
as not a part of the world, the role of theologians in the church
is not like that of theologians, poets, or philosophers in Greek
or Roman religion. It is the voice of the teaching church that
serves as the primary interpreter of Christian truth. But there is
also a need for minds that reflect on the faith and its elements,
minds that draw relationships, make distinctions, clarify meanings, and interpret texts. The function of such minds and voices
may not be directly to announce the faith but to think about it;
and such thinking, of course, always remembers that the faith
is something to be announced and lived, not something that is
most fully actualized when it is thought about. Theological
reflection is always to some extent a service.

To bring out the character of the theological voice, one further distinction should be made. Thoughtful reflection on the faith can be done by people we might call religious "essayists." The function of essayists is to bring out interesting and helpful comparisons, contrasts, clarifications, nuances, and emphases in Christian belief. In contrast, a theologian is a reflective thinker who attempts to bring out the most fundamental distinctions in the faith. One might say that a theologian tries to express truths that are more universal than those the essayist deals with, but the theological issues are more universal because they are more basic. They are distinctions and identities that rest on very few prior distinctions and identifications, or even on no prior refinements, whereas the issues raised and the points made by an essayist are several stages removed from terminal distinctions and identifications. The essayist does not intend to bring out issues beyond which one cannot move, but the theologian sets out to determine terminal distinctions and identities. In this he is analogous to the philosopher, who strives to register terminal relationships and differentiations in the world and in the human condition.

Working out terminal distinctions and their allied definitions and relationships is not simply a matter of stating facts or of repeating what others have said; it involves working with clusters of concepts and making meanings precise — it involves a raw and elementary kind of thinking. In theology it involves especially bringing out the distinction between God and the world, and the distinctions and identifications that must be clarified in respect to the incarnation and the continuing work of the Spirit in the church. Furthermore, the Christian distinctions and identifications have to be brought up against the most elementary distinctions and identifications that reason can register in the world and in the human estate; these two kinds of distinctions and identifications, the Christian and the natural, are to be identified with and differentiated from one another. In such reflective thinking one is to make room for faith within natural necessities and in contrast to them, but with full recognition of the weight of natural necessities. Such theological thinking is partly defensive, to show that Christian faith is

not incoherent or contrary to reason; it is partly an aid to the
church in maintaining its teaching and in keeping it free from
confusions and distortions; but it is also simply good as a clarification of what we believe, as a way of bringing belief forward
move vividly and with greater differentiation.

This sort of refining analysis is not the work of the teaching
church, whose primary role is to assert the Christian message
in its integrity. The authority of the theological voice comes
from knowledge and insight, and it must be able to argue for
the assertions it makes. From this point of view the medieval
disputations were an appropriate forum for theological discourse; indeed they are a better forum for theology than for
philosophical argumentation. In contrast, the authority of the
teaching church is the authority and responsibility of an office;
the church identifies and differentiates not primarily on the
basis of scholarship and reflective argument — however much it
might use these in preparing for its decision — but on its
commission to determine what is the truth of the faith. Furthermore, the theological enterprise, like all activities of the
mind, is done better by some than by others. There are figures
like Augustine, the Cappadocians, Aquinas, Scotus, and Newman, who bring out the elementary issues of the faith with such
force that they establish an intellectual age; one can hardly
work with the Christian distinctions and identifications without
taking the writings of such men into consideration, both as
examples of the best that can be done and as expressions of the
theological truth that is to be repeated. As in all endeavors of
the mind, most theological thinkers work in the shadow of
more prominent writers, but even though they are derivative
rather than originating, they are still concerned with distinctions and issues that are terminal, and in this respect they differ
from what we have called religious essayists. Finally, there are
also the historical and philological studies that make up so
much of actual theological activity and provide so much of its
material, but such studies acquire a theological form only by
being involved, ultimately, in the determination of Christian
distinctions and identifications. Without this element of
theological thinking they remain simply collections of fact and

information, whose very bulk may leave us bewildered and incapable of assimilating the materials they present.

It might seem strange, and perhaps slightly irreverent, to say that the Christian life is lived in the light of a distinction and that the Gospels narrate the events in which the Christian distinction between God and the world was most completely brought forward. Such an emphasis on a distinction may seem to make Christianity far too academic. But to be offended by this, and to think that distinctions are primarily academic matters, is to overlook the illuminating, stabilizing, and liberating activity of distinctions in life. Human life is led by distinguishing one thing from another, and it is established as human life by the possibility and by the achievement of discriminations. Distinctions are first made in the process of living; thinkers can turn to them and talk about them only because they are already there. Similarly, the basic Christian distinctions are made in Christian life — indeed Christian life is established by them — and the theological voice can speak of them only because they are already there. True, although we make distinctions in life, we may begin to talk about them reflectively and thematically in more academic settings, and so it may seem that distinctions are the property of reflective thought. Yet such a claim to ownership is not fair to the original possessor of the distinction, the life in which the distinction is first made, and it gives a distorted view of how distinctions exist. It also fails to see how the academic treatment of distinctions should illuminate what occurs in life. Distinctions make human life possible, and, more profoundly, the Christian distinction between God and the world makes possible the life of man with God that has been given to us in Christ.

NOTE

1. The church's activity of discriminating between the essential and the circumstantial is brought out by Jean Levie, S.J., in *The Bible, Word of God in Words of Men*, translated by S.H. Treman (New York:

P.J. Kennedy, 1962), p. 216: "Many passages in Scripture thus presuppose a concrete and temporary situation (which no longer exists) in terms of which an authoritative solution was given by the prophet, apostle, or inspired writer. The individual exegete often feels he is incompetent to separate the definitive from the temporary and the contingent. These cases are among those which most stress the need for a Church to be the constant interpreter of Scripture throughout the ages."

4. The Incarnation and the Christian Distinction

In pagan religion and philosophy distinctions are made within the context of the world or the whole, the matrix of being in which one thing comes forward as differentiated from others. Sameness and otherness are at work within a setting that is ultimate. This setting for distinctions is not, in turn, identified against or differentiated from anything beyond itself. Reason works within this whole; it may be able to disclose the various substantial necessities proper to things within the whole, and it may even be able to reach necessities that are proper to the whole as encompassing, but these are the limits that it pushes against in the extremity of its thinking (Timaeus 36D – 37C). If reason tries to consider that which permits these necessities themselves, it touches on what Plato is said to have named the One and its inevitable Indeterminate Dyad, the power of divergence that must always also be there as a condition for the necessities that we can reason about.

In Christian belief the world or the whole itself is placed as one of the terms of a distinction. The novelty of this gesture and the unusual character of this distinction must not be underestimated. The normal and direct distinguishing and identifying power of reason is exercised within the context of the world or the whole, and the names and syntax that are at home within such a context must be properly adjusted if they are to function in the new horizon which now includes reason's normal setting as a subordinated part. In addition the speaker who tries to think and speak in the new context appears to be projected beyond his normal surroundings, and questions become raised

for him about the necessity of what had seemed to him the way
things inexorably had to be.

It is not just that things could have been very different from
the way they are; we are now to speak of things, and of the
whole, as possibly not having been at all. And we are to speak
of ourselves as possibly not having been at all. These
"possibilities" are very unlike the possibilities we usually deal
with, like the possibility of snow tomorrow, the possibility of
losing one's job, the possibility of moving against gravity, and
the possibility of an answer to a particular mathematical problem. It is not as simple as one might suppose it is to think the
possibility of things' not being at all, and also not simple to
think our own not being at all. And finally, as a kind of closure
to the distinction between God and the world, we are to think
of the possibility of things' not being, and of our own not being,
in such a way that there is no less goodness or greatness — not
"in the world," obviously, but "there" at all. This last, "closing" qualification, that there be no diminution of goodness and
greatness, might seem like a supplement added to the earlier
conceptions that things might not have existed and that we
might not have existed; but it is not a mere supplement, because the thought that things and we ourselves, as a whole,
might not have been, did in fact not come about except in the
new light of the Christian conception of the Good and the One.
The thought that things generally, and we ourselves, might not
have existed is bearable — bearable not just emotionally but as
a conceivability — only against the other term of this distinction, the term that must be so understood that even if nothing
else did exist, there would be no diminution of excellence.

When we so turn away from the world or from the whole
and turn toward God, toward the other term of the distinction
that comes to light in Christian belief, we begin to appreciate
the strangeness of the distinction itself. In the distinctions that
occur normally within the setting of the world, each term distinguished is what it is precisely by not being that which it is
distinguishable from. Its being is established partially by its
otherness, and therefore its being depends on its distinction
from others. But in the Christian distinction God is understood

as "being" God entirely apart from any relation of otherness to the world or to the whole. God could and would be God even if there were no world. Thus the Christian distinction is appreciated as a distinction that did not have to be, even though it in fact is. The most fundamental thing we come to in Christianity, the distinction between the world and God, is appreciated as not being the most fundamental thing after all, because one of the terms of the distinction, God, is more fundamental than the distinction itself.

In Christian faith God is understood not only to have created the world, but to have permitted the distinction between himself and the world to occur. He is not established as God by the distinction (whereas pagan gods are established by being different than other things). No distinction made within the horizon of the world is like this, and therefore the act of creation cannot be understood in terms of any action or any relationship that exists in the world. The special sense of sameness in God "before" and "after" creation, and the special sense of otherness between God and the world, impose qualifications on whatever we are to say about God and the world, about creation out of nothing, about God's way of being present and interior to things and yet beyond them. All the names and syntax we use for such theological discourse have to be adapted from their normal use in the element of the identities and differences within the world. Furthermore, if "being" is the term that philosophers use to name that which is articulated in the sameness and otherness that reason can register, if "being" is used for the world as last horizon, it is appropriate that another term, like "*esse*," be introduced for use in the "whole" made up of God and the world, as a name for what is articulated in the identities and differences occuring in this new context.

The Christian distinction between God and the world is therefore a distinction that is, in principle, both most primary and yet capable of being obliterated, because one of the terms of the distinction, the world, does not have to be. To be God, God does not need to be distinguished from the world, because there does not need to be anything other than God alone. As

Aquinas has formulated it, God is not related by a real relation
to the world.[1] This should not be taken psychologically, it
should not be taken in terms of human emotions, and it does
not mean that God is unconcerned with the world; it describes
how God exists. And the world is not diminished in its own
excellence, it is not somehow slighted because God is not related by a real relation to it; rather the world is now understood as not having had to be. If it did not have to be, it is
there out of a choice. And if the choice was not motivated by
any need of completion in the one who let it be, and not even
motivated by the need for "there" to be more perfection and
greatness, then the world is there through an incomparable
generosity. The world exists simply for the glory of God. The
glory of God is seen not only in particularly splendid parts of
the world but in the very existence of the world and everything
in it.

It is remarkable that among the many issues that arose as
serious controversies in the history of the church, the issue of
creation and the relationship between God and the world has
been far less conspicuous than other questions, like those dealing with Christ and his actions, with grace, with the sacraments, and with the church. It is as though the Christian understanding of God and the world provides the setting that lets
there be controversies about Christ, the church, and grace.
However, it is also the case that various heresies concerning
such issues are heretical because they would, by implication,
obscure the Christian distinction between the world and God.
The Christian understanding of God and the world is not an
inert background for more controversial issues; it enters into
their formulation and helps determine how they must be
decided.

The issue the church had to settle first, once it acquired
public and official recognition under Constantine and could
turn to controversies regarding its teaching, was the issue concerning the being and the actions of Christ. There were controversies regarding Jesus even during the first three centuries
of the church, but they became open and explicit in the Arian
heresy and the arguments that followed. They were treated in

the Councils of Nicaea, Constantinople, Ephesus, and Chalcedon. One can never say with assurance that history has to develop along certain lines, but it does seem inevitable that the first topic the church would have to clarify, somehow or other, was the way in which Jesus existed and the effect his actions had.

Among the many intepretations that were proposed, some held that the Logos was not fully divine, that is, not completely equal to God the Father but somehow subordinated to him; and others held that when the Logos assumed human existence, he assumed a human nature that was incomplete in some way or other: lacking a soul, for example, or lacking the rational part of the soul. In determining these issues in their various stages, the Church maintained that although Jesus is one person and one agent, the Son of God, he is fully divine and fully human. Because he is fully human, each of his actions was integrally human, even while being the actions of a divine person. As the Council of Chalcedon states, "We teach . . . that one and the same Christ, the Son, the Lord, the Only-Begotten is to be recognized in two natures without mixture, without transformation, without division, without separation; the difference of the natures being in no way abrogated through the unification; the properties of each nature remaining, rather, preserved" (*Denzinger*, 148). Thus for the unity of the incarnation it was not necessary that the human nature of Jesus be diminished and replaced, in part, by the divine. The two natures remain completely what they are. Furthermore, it is not the case that some of the actions of Jesus were divine and not human, like his transfiguration or his miracles or his forgiveness of sins, while other actions were human and not divine, like his becoming tired or hungry or his conversing with other people. All his actions, as well as his being, were integrally human and yet divine, because they were the human actions of a divine agent.

The Council of Chalcedon, and the councils and controversies that led up to it, were concerned with the mystery of Christ, but they also tell us about the God who became incarnate in Christ. They tell us first that God does not destroy the natural necessities of things he becomes involved with, even in the intimate union of the incarnation. What is according to nature, and what reason can disclose in nature, retains its integrity before the Christian God. And second, they tell us that we must think of God as the one who can let natural necessity be maintained and let reason be left intact: that is, God is not himself a competing part of nature or a part of the world. If the incarnation could not take place without a truncation of human nature, it would mean that God was one of the natures in the world that somehow was defined by not being the other natures; it would mean that his presence in one of these other natures, human nature, would involve a conflict and a need to exclude some part of what he is united with. Either God would only seem to have become man, or he would have become united to something less than man and would have become a new kind of being in the world. These are all ways in which the pagans thought the gods could take on human form or bring about beings that were higher than the race of men but lower than the gods. The reason the pagans could not conceive of anything like the incarnation is that their gods are part of the world, and the union of any two natures in the world is bound to be, in some way, unnatural, because of the otherness that lets one thing be itself only by not being the other. But the Christian God is not a part of the world and is not a "kind" of being at all. Therefore the incarnation is not meaningless or impossible or destructive.

The Christological heresies are a reflection of tendencies to make pagan the Christian sense of the divine. These tendencies do not stem only from the social and educational milieu of the early centuries of Christian history; they are part of the normal tendency of reason to situate itself within the world and its necessities and to define everything within that context. This inclination is still with us now and will be with us always. It inevitably introduces tensions between itself and Christian belief. It is an inclination Christians must be aware of, an inclination against which Christian theological thinking must be differentiated. To consider the early Christological controversies and their attendant councils as merely historical episodes, or to suppose that they are just an importation of Hellenistic thought-patterns into Christianity, is to fail to take seriously the need to distinguish Christian faith and its theology from simply natural religion and philosophy.

The main focus of the early councils, those actions in which the church determined how its biblical message was to be repeated in the post-biblical age, was on the being and the actions of Jesus. However, by implication, the church also determined its understanding of God and of the relationship between God and the world. The concentration on Christ made more vivid the setting against which the mystery of Christ was to be stated. The Christian distinction between God and the world, the denial that God in his divinity is part of or dependent on the world, was brought forward with greater clarity through the discussion of the way the Word became flesh. The same distinction was also emphasized as a background for the Trinitarian doctrines and for the controversies about grace. If human agency could, on its own terms, achieve or at least initiate the divine life in man, as the Pelagians and Semi-Pelagians held, then that divine life would be something achievable within the powers of nature and the world, and God would not be distinguished from the world in the way Christian faith understands him to be. Thus many of the crucial dogmatic issues raised in the early centuries of the church engage the question of the relationship between God and the world, and the positions judged to be erroneous would generally have obscured the Christian distinction between the divine and the mundane.

But looking at it from the other perspective, the Christian distinction between God and the world serves to permit the other Christian mysteries to be thought as mysteries and not as incoherences. The Christian understanding of God is necessary to open the space within which the other Christian mysteries can be believed. After Ephesus and Chalcedon we can say that Jesus is one person or one agent and that there are two natures in him, but these statements do not explain the mystery of Christ. In fact, we are familiar only with agents who act according to their own single nature, and if we were to try to think of two complete mundane natures as forming one being, we would find it self-contradicting and unthinkable. Only if the

divine is not one of the natures in the world can the incarnation, and the salvation it achieved, occur; only then can the
church assert the special kind of identity and difference that it
maintains took place in the being and the life of Jesus. Ephesus
and Chalcedon presuppose this understanding of God. The
councils do not explain away the mystery, but neither do they
just stipulate how Christians are to talk or not to talk about
Christ. The councils do not merely set down verbal conventions. They allow the mystery to remain a mystery. They
prevent the mystery from dissolving into incoherence, and they
also prevent it from falling back into being a simple natural
phenomenon. Some understanding of the mystery as a mystery
is needed to keep it alive in this way. The councils could not
have succeeded in preserving the mystery of the incarnation
and redemption except against the setting of the Christian understanding of God and the world.

The same is true of other Christian mysteries. One could
not assert that there are three persons in one nature if the
nature were taken as one of the natures in the world, one of
the kinds of beings that exist only by being contrasted to other
kinds. The life of grace could not be admitted if it were to be
taken as another human achievement in tension with the emotional, psychological, ethical, political, and cognitive activities of
human nature. The sacraments could not do what Christians
believe they accomplish if their special sacramental activity
were just one more mundane kind of representation or depic-
tion or symbolization added to the ways in which other signs
function in the world. Unless the Christian sense of the divine
is differentiated from anything and everything in the being of
the world, unless the Christian God is differentiated from what
philosophers have called the whole, all the Christian mysteries
cease to be mysteries. Either they become impossibilities, or
they become accommodated to natural necessities, or they are
made to compete with what is natural and to obfuscate the way
things have to be. The Christian distinction between God and
the world allows the formulations of the other mysteries to say
something and prevents them from shattering as statements.

If the Christian understanding of God and the world is the

condition for our ability to assert the other Christian mysteries as mysteries, then this understanding is different from the other mysteries. Is it also a mystery itself? It is an understanding that in fact becomes available in faith, in Christian life and action, and in connection with the other mysteries of the faith. But when we reflect on the distinction between God and the world, there is a kind of reasonable appreciation possible that is not available in the other mysteries, which are beyond reason. The negations, identifications, and differentiations at work in this fundamental Christian distinction are very much adjusted from their normal way of working within the horizon of the world or the whole, but there is a touch of clarity for us, and indeed for everyone, in them. As St. Anselm says, even the *insipiens* can appreciate that something is being said in the definition of what God is. There is something like negation at work here, there is something analogous to identification and to differentiation, and there is a kind of focus on the whole or the world. This distinction is not simply one more rational insight that anyone who fully uses his mind should accomplish, but it is also not a distinction that is totally opaque. The formulation of this distinction is not an agglomeration of words that has no sense. The distinction is glimpsed on the margin of reason, and because of the importance it has for belief in the other Christian mysteries and for the Christian life generally, it may be said to be at the intersection of reason and faith. Because of it the Christian faith remains faith, but a reasoned faith.

The direct focus of the teaching of the church is on the life, actions, and words of Jesus. The good news of the Gospels is that God has become man and that he has made it possible for human beings to share in the life of God. This is seen to be a gift that no one could have anticipated or demanded, a gift that was not necessitated by anything in the nature of things. But the generosity of the incarnation is seen against another generosity and another gift, the act of creation, which was also done out of no compulsion and no need: "*mirabiliter condidisti et mirabilius reformasti*; you have wonderfully established and yet more wonderfully renewed." The act of creation does not bring in its train the necessity of the incarnation, so the presence of

God among human beings is doubly generous; but the sense of creation, the sense of the distinction between God and the world, becomes more fully visible to us in the light of the incarnation and the salvation brought to us when God became man.

NOTE

1. See *Summa theologiae* I q. 13, art. 7, c; q. 28, art 1, ad 3; *De veritate* q. 4, art. 5, c; q. 3, art. 3, c.

5. The Metaphysics of Christian Belief

The Christian sense of God and the world was elaborated in the metaphysics of St. Thomas Aquinas. He speaks of God as *ipsum esse subsistens* and describes all other beings as existing through a participation in *esse*. Aquinas thinks of beings in a context very much different from the final context Aristotle and Plato and other pagan philosophers acknowledged; Aquinas thinks of beings over against their sheer nonexistence, over against the nonexistence of the world or the whole, whereas pagan thinkers thought of things as being or not being within the whole. Aquinas considers the existence of things to be an actuality, an actuality determined by what the thing in each case is. Any given thing is not a sheer actuality, but an actuality of a special kind. The kind or essence lets the actuality occur, but it also confines the actuality to existing only in its particular way. The essence, as a potentiality to exist, allows something to *be* this sort of thing, but it also allows it to be only *this sort* of thing. Any particular being is actual and therefore has the perfection of existing, but it can be actual only because it must be contented to be within certain limits. Each thing is allowed to have its perfections because it is what it is, but the very possession of such perfections is at the same time the exclusion of the perfections of other kinds of things: a tree is not and cannot be a man, a dog is not and cannot be a diamond. This exclusion is characteristic of all "limited" beings. Their act of existence, their *esse*, is confined by what they are, by their essence, to being only this kind of existent.

But God is the sheer act of *esse subsistens*, the sheer act of

existing. He is not confined to being this kind of thing as opposed to that kind. He is not a "kind" of thing at all, only sheer
esse. Does the unqualified act of *esse* exclude the act of existing
as a man? Or the act of existing as an animal? Or the act of
existing as a tree? In the Thomistic understanding this kind of
question is inappropriate. Between God and creatures there is
no exclusion like the exclusion among finite beings.[1] Creatures
each exist in a certain way, whereas God is pure existence.
Whatever goodness or greatness occurs in creatures occurs
therefore in an eminent way in God. Hence after creation there
are more beings but not more perfection of *esse*.

Creatures then are limited in two ways: they are limited in
relation to one another and they are limited in relation to God.
These two limitations are different. We experience the first, the
limitation of one being against another, in our natural experience. We differentiate ourselves from other things and we distinguish one thing from another; we do this in experiences that
range from highly emotional, competitive, or tragic encounters,
to cool, detached analyses, but always our negations and exclu-
sions are responses to the presentation of differences in which
two things emerge as other to each other. But the second kind
of limitation, that between creatures and God, does not intrude
on us in the same way. There is no special experience that
actually presents to us the difference between God and the
world (since all experience takes place within the world). The
difference between God and the world is appreciated, not felt,
and it does not exercise on our perception the sort of emotional pull that the divine exercises on the pagan awareness. If
we were to feel or perceive the difference between God and the
world, God would have become introduced as one of the differentiated kinds in the world, one of the beings that is distinguished from others, as indeed the pagan divinity was thought
to be.

The Thomistic metaphysics of *esse* is worked out in the context of God as sheer existence and the world, with all its beings, as possibly not existing. This context is different from the
setting for Aristotelian metaphysics, if we may take Aristotle as
representative of pagan thinking. Even the sense in which be-

ings are differentiated from one another is different in the two thinkers. Aristotle talks about what a thing is, but he really does not speak about the essence of a thing as Thomas understands essence. For Aristotle being is centralized or unified into this thing or that; the thing's being is its being presentable as one thing over against the others it is differentiated from. The thing emerges as a center of performance and intelligibility. But this play of determination and opposition occurs against the setting of the whole; it is the actualization of what can come into prominence within the whole. It is not the actualization of this being in contrast to its not existing at all. "Existing," or *esse*, is for Aristotle not a theme for thought, and indeed it becomes a theme for thought only within the special historical tradition of Christian belief.

One of the issues that becomes critical in Christian thinking is the relationship between God and the natures or essences of things created. Because all creatures exist through God's choice, a dilemma seems to follow: either created natures are inherently arbitrary, and things seem to lose their natural necessity; or created natures are somehow integral and determined apart from God's will, at least in their potentiality to be what they are, and God's creative power seems to be confined by something outside himself. Are natures what they are because God chooses them to be structured so and so, or are they what they are somehow in themselves? For example, is respect for parents good because God decrees it to be good, or does God have to acknowledge it as good because it is somehow in the nature of the relationship between parents and children? Is man a being capable of speech because God decrees it so, or does God have to accept man this way because man simply would not be man without the power of speech? If things are what they are by divine choice, then natures or essences seem to be drained of their necessity. But if the necessity of natures and essences is left intact, is not God ruled by patterns over against himself? Does not being have its own compulsion, at least in its possibilities, and does not God's creative power become simply the power of giving actuality to some things and not to others?

This question is of both speculative and practical importance. It affects the attitudes a Christian will have toward the
natures of things and the way he will behave in regard to them.
If created natures are inherently arbitrary, our recognition of
them is merely provisional. Things could have been very different from what they are, so what they are seems quite dispensa-
ble. The true nature and the true reality is then a will, and not
the way things are. Even our recognition of the excellences of
created natures may become utilitarian; we see their excellence,
not as a good in itself, but as a good in view of a good beyond
them. It seems that the excellence of created natures could
have been replaced by quite another excellence as long as the
good beyond them were well served. On the other hand, someone with a vivid sense of the integrity and excellence of the
natures of things may be tempted to think that the notion of a
creator is incoherent if it somehow undermines the necessity
that reason brings out in the way things are. The necessity in
things seems to limit the omnipotence of God. We seem to be
left with a dilemma between arbitrariness that appears to
undercut necessity and necessity that appears to dominate the
creator. The dilemma arises because the world with its necessities is positioned within the context of creation, and it can be
resolved only if we clarify how the new context is to be understood.

Aquinas discusses this issue in terms of what he calls the
"ideas" in God. Aquinas says that there are such ideas or forms
in God and that they serve as the exemplars according to which
things are created. He insists that the ideas do not split up the
simplicity of the divine intellect because they are the divine *esse*
as it can be imitated or participated in by other beings. God
essentially knows himself, and in doing so he knows the others
that can be by virtue of himself: "As God knows his essence as
so imitable by such a creature, he knows it as the particular
model (*ratio*) and idea of that creature."[2] These metaphysical
and theological remarks of Aquinas do not imply that God is unconcerned with anything besides himself. For creatures exist
precisely as participations in the divine *esse*, and by knowing
them this way God knows them more intimately than they can

be known by anyone who becomes acquainted with them apart from their relationship to God. God's knowledge of creatures through himself is a knowledge of what is deeper in them than the natures, features, and properties we come to know through our cognitive involvement with them; their being known and chosen by God is what is most real in them. We may dimly appreciate their relationship with God through our faith and through the glimpse of createdness our thinking may catch sight of, but we never perceive this relationship clearly and directly, and still less do we see that in God of which these beings are the external participations.

Through his doctrine of the divine ideas Aquinas avoids the alternative between natures arbitrarily constructed and natures determined independently of God. "What things are" retains its necessity because the essences of things are the ways *esse* can be determined, but *esse* subsists only in God, so the basis for the determination of things is not distinct from him: it is his own existence. The potentiality for there to be various kinds of things is to be placed, not in any material or foundation distinct from God, but in God himself. A problem analogous to this was, of course, formulated by Plato in the *Euthyphro*, where Socrates asks whether things that are good are loved by the gods because they are good or whether they become good by being loved by the gods. However, Plato is concerned with the problems that arise when nature is distinguished from myth and convention; he is not asking about the relationship between the world as created and God as creator.

Theological reflection on creation has to become engaged with philosophical reflection on the world or the whole. What philosophy has to say about the whole and its necessities is the province of first, or ultimate, philosophy, and it might seem undesirable to have to relate theological thinking to such distant and "airy" speculation. But the issue of the whole is not as distant and idle as it might seem; even in ordinary understanding we all have opinions about the whole. They might be an extrapolation of some form of "science," as science is institutionalized in our world, or they might be a "world-view" we have from our upbringing, our religion, and our culture.

Such views about the whole, and on being human as a special
part of the whole, are notoriously vague and ambiguous, and
philosophy is the attempt to think as explicitly and appropriately as we can about the whole. In pagan philosophy and religion the world is there as the matrix and setting for all the
particular issues that more directly engage our attention.
Christian belief in creation makes the world or the whole explicitly thematic because it urges a special kind of negation of
the world or the whole; it urges a distinction between the
whole and God.

One danger in this is that the world might lose its character
as a matrix and ultimate setting and begin to look like a large
thing, a global object, instead of being taken as a setting for
things and objects; this would occur if the distinction between
God and the world is misread as one of the distinctions we
naturally and spontaneously make between things within the
world. This misunderstanding of both the world and God, this
taking of both of them as new kinds of objects, can be prevented by a proper emphasis on the philosophical inquiry into
the whole and its necessities; by an awareness of the special
sense of God as *ipsum esse subsistens* and the special transformation of language that occurs when we begin to speak, religiously
and theologically, about God; and by an explicit study of the
unusual character of the distinction between the whole and
God. But despite the danger of misunderstanding, Christian
theology inevitably engages philosophy, the study of the whole,
by virtue of the special kind of distinction, negation, or separation that Christian belief executes in regard to being and the
whole. This unsettled and unsettling relationship between theology and philosophy — and philosophy itself is a kind of extreme and unsettling human preoccupation — has been one of
the major causes of motion in Western civilization.

The pagan sense of the divine is that of the best, highest,
greatest, most powerful and most necessary beings within the
whole or within the world. There are bound to be many different conceptions of the highest and first substance, depending on
what approach is used to come to it. It can be described as the
pervasive life-force of the world, as the Stoics described it; or

as pure thinking; or as a cause of motion; or as a comprehensive and final architectonic force; or as some sort of ultimately necessary being in the world. If the approach to the ultimate is more anthropomorphic and less philosophical, the divine may be described in terms of human power, antiquity, or wisdom. If it is conceived in terms of a people or nation, it will have features related to that community and its history. There are competing notions of the ultimate substance because it is a special kind of being with a special involvement with other beings. Even pagan monotheisms have different interpretations of the divine, conditioned by the cultures in which they arise, and calling for fusions and conflicts of interpretations when, through either peaceful exchanges or war, these senses of the divine enter into contact with one another.

In contrast, such diversities do not occur to the Christian sense of God precisely because it is defined, not by contrast to other beings in the world, but in contrast to the world as the whole. No "kinds" of things, cultural or substantial, reach beyond the setting of the world to determine the proper names we are to give to the Christian God; God is primarily sheer *esse*, not pure thinking, life, or power. There is a more radical unity and identity in the Christian God, and consequently a greater universality: he is not the God of a particular nation or culture. In principle the fusion and conflict of interpretations between the Christian sense of God and the sense of the divine in particular cultures is not the same as the fusion and conflict of the senses of the divine proper to various cultures. Christian missionary activity does not have to impose a culture and eradicate the human way of life that is already in place in order to tell about God and his creative and redemptive action. God is not simply the greatest being in the world or the highest principle in a world-view; he is understood as distinguished from the world and from any world-view.

But although the Christian God is not one of the gods of the nations or one of the gods of the philosophers, a special identification of the Christian God with what people worship is possible once the Christian setting is reached. The Christian sense of God is not a new definition of the best and greatest being, a definition that enters into conflict with others: God is understood as distinct from the world, not the best thing in it. Once this new context is reached, new "kinds" of differences become available which were not available within the setting of the whole, and an identification can take place in these differences that could not take place in the philosophical or naturally religious setting. To attempt to identify, say, the Stoic god with the Zeus of Homer and Hesiod, or with Aristotle's unmoved mover, or with the god of another culture and tradition, is not like saying that what the pagans seek in their unknown god is the God that Christians worship (Acts 17:22 – 34). The identifications are different because the differences within which the identifications are made are different. The Christian questioning of the world establishes contrasts that do not enter into the fusion of various cultural and religious horizons. The Christian sense of God is, not simply a human or religious improvement on other senses of the divine, but a new kind of completion that does not appear as a possibility in simply natural religion and philosophy. Natural religion is fulfilled more radically in Christianity than it expects to be fulfilled; but what is natural in it is completed, not destroyed, by the Christian dimension.

Of course this fulfillment is visible as a fulfillment only from the setting established by Christian belief, and only if the distinctions proper to that setting are appreciated. Otherwise Christianity is taken as yet another cultural form, as a tribal or a political religion, and its sense of God is interpreted within the horizon of natural religion, within the horizon of the world or the whole, with destructive consequences for Christianity and for nature. But if the Christian distinction is correctly appreciated and correctly lived, then the cultural forms in which it is realized, the habits, music, language, gestures, work and social order, the nuances of moral life and of human relationships, can be brought forward in their own excellence and still be in the service of Christian faith. Christian belief has to be saturated with cultural forms if it is to be publicly alive, but it is never inseparable from a particular culture, the way the gods of a people or the gods of a city may be. This fusion and distinguishability of culture and Christian faith is based ultimately on the sense of God made present in Christianity. Christian faith also promotes love for one's people and country, obedience to the laws, and the pursuit of justice, those virtues that the gods of the tribe or the city are to foster; but the Christian faith is never solely confined to this public function of religion, because the God worshipped in faith is never the god of the tribe or the city. Obviously there are instances of distortion and confusion in these matters, and some forms of Christian religion may in fact have been reduced to principles for national patriotism or to ideological justifications for laws that exist in a particular polity; and perhaps some Christian sects or communities have taken on too intense a national coloration. But like all important distinctions, the Christian distinction is not easy to live. It demands discrimination and prudence, especially of persons in authority and those who set the public tone. No technique or methodology can ever replace good judgment in determining how to clarify obscurities and resolve ambiguous issues in such matters. Even theological accuracy is not sufficient to indicate how decisions and actions should proceed. But the obscurities and ambiguities are precisely the obfuscation of a distinction that can in principle be adequately made in whatever circumstances may at the moment prevail.

Historically, one of the most important confrontations between the pagan and Christian senses of the world and the divine took place in the conflict in the thirteenth century between Christian theology and Averroistic versions of Aristotle. Aristotle became known to European Christians for the first time in a massive way through the translations and commentaries that were made of his works in that period. Because of his teachings on the eternity of the world and his silence about creation, Aristotle was considered a threat to Christian belief, at least until his thought was assimilated into the work of Thomas Aquinas and other thinkers. The Christian tradition has, however, generally thought of the Platonic form of philosophy as more congenial to its own convictions; the *Timaeus* was known, in part, to Christians for centuries before the beginnings of scholasticism, and Aquinas even mentions Plato's account of creation as being an interpretation of the book of

Genesis.[3] However, for Christian belief to assimilate and to distinguish itself from Platonism may in fact be more difficult than for it to come to terms with Aristotle. Just because of the propinquity, the contrasts may be harder to draw. Aristotle's god is so clearly a "first substance" within the world that the difference between his teaching and Christianity is obvious to almost every reader. But Plato goes beyond substances, even first substances, in his philosophical analysis of the whole; he comes to the One or the Good as something beyond things and being, something that still has an effect on particular beings or forms of appearance and lets them be and appear as what they are, while always receding from a direct presentation of itself in any particular. There is a sense of the One as the beneficent center of things, the object of almost religious reverence. Plato's formulas about this, through the neoplatonic tradition they later entered, were frequently adopted by Christian thinkers to express what they meant by God and the world's relation to him. In recent years Heidegger's writings about *Sein* and *Ereignis*, issues that are not foreign to what Plato discusses on the extreme margin of philosophy, have provoked a similar response.

But the Christian sense of God must be "distinguished" from issues such as these. God is not the ever elusive but ever involved oneness, the steady pivot that lets the plays of presence and absence, and sameness and otherness, and rest and motion, occur in the beings and the forms of presentation we encounter. This oneness or goodness is what thinking catches glimpses of when it reaches the edge of rational order and tries to think about what lets the order be: but *this* letting be is not creation. Perhaps the Platonic oneness and the dyadic divergence that is always played off against it were obscured as themes for thought because of the theological brilliance of creation; but Heidegger's statement of these issues, and the emphasis many writers have placed recently on relation and opposition as prior even to substance, demand that the Christian sense of God and creation be more explicitly differentiated from these things that appear so much like it. Even mysticism, if considered a form of experience appropriate to approaching the center of things, is not necessarily or exclusively related to Christianity, nor can Christianity be judged by the criterion of its potential for mysticism. There is an other dimension beyond being and reason, and it is acknowledged by Plato, but it is not the same as the transcendence of God appreciated in Christian faith. It would be interesting to draw the distinction between Platonic and Christian elements in the works of writers like the Pseudo-Dionysius, Ruysbroeck, and Meister Eckhart. There are difficulties in making contrasts here because the sense of one-ness we find in Plato is itself reached only by the most refined and angled expression, as Heidegger has shown when he treats these issues in some of his later writings, and it is reached as a *nec plus ultra* for language.[4] But the Christian God is not simply a *plus ultra*, something yet more distant but in the same direc-tion; the Christian God is not, for example, the One as separate from the Indeterminate Dyad, nor the One projected to a more intense degree of unity. The Christian sense of the divine is simply and entirely another issue. But what does "other" mean at this extreme, and how can it be brought out? Must one, theologically, somehow go "through" the One and the Inde-terminate Dyad to come to the Christian sense of God? These are topics for theological reflection, in which the Christian sense of God is to be distinguished not only from natural necessities but from the oneness and goodness that permit such necessities to be what they are and to appear as they do.[5]

NOTES

1. See St. Thomas Aquinas, *In librum Beati Dionysii De Divinis Nominibus expositio* (Rome: Marietti, 1950), § 661, p. 245: "Non enim esse suum est finitum per aliquam naturam determinatam ad genus vel speciem, ut possit dici quod *est hoc* et *non est* illud, ut sunt deter-minatae etiam substantiae spirituales." On God as *esse subsistens* and creatures as limited, see *De potentia* q. 1, art. 2, c; q. 7, art. 2, ad 6; ad 9; *Summa theologiae* I q. 4, art. 2, c.

2. *Summa theologiae* I q. 15, art. 3. See all of q. 15; see q. 14, art. 5;

and q. 44, art 3: "Whether the exemplary cause is anything beyond God."

3. *De potentia* q. 4, art. 1, ad 2. See also his *Scriptum super libros sententiarum Magistri Petri Lombardi*, Book I, dist. III, q. 1, art. 4, ad 1: "Plato autem dicitur multa cognovisse de divinis, legens in libris veteris legis, quos invenit in Aegypto."

4. For an excellent discussion of Heidegger and Christian theology see Hans Urs von Balthasar, *Herrlichkeit: eine theologische Aesthetik,* vol. 3, 1 (Einsiedeln: Johannes Verlag, 1965), pp. 769 – 86. For a treatment of related topics, see Robert Sokolowski, *Presence and Absence* (Bloomington: Indiana University Press, 1978), chapter 15.

5. In making these remarks we ourselves are now speaking about such distinctions and contrasts; we are not effectively making them. To do so is the task of theological thinking in its most profound and original form.

6. Natural Virtue

The natural necessities that present themselves to reason with their own evidence, and that retain their integrity in the theological context, include such things as the laws of material nature, the biological patterns of existence that make up the reality of living things, the various forms of presentation and the relationships among them, the patterns of psychological development, and the social, political, and economic structures of human association. But natural necessities also include the elements and structures of human action, and in particular they include that which makes human action good or bad. It is possible to make distinctions and definitions that clarify what human action is and what virtue and vice are. Such clarifications are especially important when human action is placed within the Christian setting, when natural virtue must be differentiated from Christian theological virtue and vice differentiated from sin. We must also determine to what extent people act, to what extent they exist as agents, in the Christian setting. Just as the Christian sense of God is best appreciated in contrast to the achievements of natural reason and pagan religion, so the sense of Christian action, the sense of how we can conduct ourselves in the space opened by Christian faith, is best determined in contrast with natural human agency.

The problem is heightened because in general the word "action," and related terms like "responsibility" and "authority," do not have a clear sense for us. There are philosophical, economic, social, political, scientific, and ideological reasons for this uncertainty; the very scale of society makes us cynical about the reality of action, since so many events we are aware of seem to move in waves so large that they are beyond anyone's deliberation and choice. And if we cannot make a difference, we cannot be said to have acted. This felt uneasiness is reflected in two opposite ideological extremes: some simply deny there can be anything like agency or responsibility, while others trivialize action. Not being able to act, they make a virtue out of a compulsion and say that the pathetic gestures they are reduced to are in fact what we should call human action. Action is equated with being in motion — whether emotionally, spatially, or verbally — or with idle, symbolic gestures that determine nothing, or with rhetorical performances. This oscillation between ideological extremes, between the deterministic and the romantic, is related to an interpretation of reason as overly "mathematical," as detached from appraisal and choice in the world in which we live: over against such mathematical reason, "responsibility" is left either to lurch willfully from one thing to another or merely to implement the unquestionable, inevitable designs of thought.

Our theological and philosophical purposes require that we bring out to some extent the nature of human action, as well as the nature of virtue and vice. To do this we will especially make use of Aristotle, and we will develop aspects of his ethical teaching that are not sufficiently recognized. Aristotle wrote about human action at the time when nature was first explicitly differentiated from convention, when human agency was distinguished from divine, almost animistic forces, and when reason was distinguished from unquestioned opinion. The natural condition of human agency stands out more vividly in such an initial demarcation. Paradoxically, the very achievement of Aristotle and other philosophers becomes a kind of public possession that serves to occlude the phenomenon it is meant to illuminate; attention is drawn to the text, the text may be misinterpreted, and the nature it is supposed to clarify becomes instead obscured. An effort is required to make Aristotle's text simpler for us and to make the moral phenomena he describes present again. Furthermore, our way of thinking about moral issues is very much influenced by the way Kant formulated

them. Kant was influenced by Christian moral teaching and by
currents in modernity that tend toward the overly formal, detached sense of reason we have mentioned above. To get at
natural moral phenomena we must get out from under Kant,
and away from his formulations of moral terms and alterna-
tives; Aristotle can help us do so.

The discussion of morals is not unrelated to a theological
reflection on the sense of the divine. One of the factors that
becomes reinterpreted when the sense of the divine changes is
the nature of human conduct. When pagan myths and religions
gave way to the philosophical discrimination between nature
and convention, human agency was also seen in a new light; or,
to put it in an equivalently accurate form, when human agency
became interpreted philosophically, nature and convention
became dissociated. These dimensions of the whole are so intimately related that no single one of them can be shifted without adjusting the others, and it is idle even to ask which dimension is clarified first or which affects the others. They all
take on new placements together. Likewise, when the pagan
setting of nature, the gods, action, and the whole become il-
luminated by the Christian sense of nature as created and God
as creator, man becomes called to act in a very different context; or, again conversely, the call for repentance, faith, hope,
and charity, the new announcement of salvation, this provoca-
tion to act in a new way, implies a different sense of the divine
and the world. We do not learn about the Christian sense of
God apart from learning about a new way of acting to which
we are called, and we do not learn about salvation apart from
learning of the new sense of God. But what does human conduct mean in this new setting? How does it differ from what
the philosophers described when they took their difference
from the poets?

In fact the phenomenon of the divine occurs to us only with
the concurrence of human agency. The divine is inseparable
from a sense of the good and the obligatory, and if we persuade
ourselves that we do not act, if we interpret being in such a
way that we acknowledge no agency in it, we also conceal from
ourselves the sense of god or the gods. There is an element of

agency even in thinking: there is responsibility in being truthful, in letting things appear as they are. But if we drain ourselves of agency, the "reason" that is left over in us is merely the reason of calculation or puzzle-solving; it does not respond to the good and it does not disclose the divine. This is not to say that we infer the existence of gods from the fact of human freedom; that would be to stand outside our own responsibility and to see it as something caused by another. The relationship we are describing is one of disclosure, not inference: responsibility is a factor in the disclosure of the divine. The divine appears only to a dative that acts, and the ambience of action is required to let the divine appear. If we turn ourselves into idle calculators, the divine appears, if at all, only as a function that brings things to an elegant closure. It is easy to dismiss the divine if we persuade ourselves that we do not, indeed cannot, assume any responsibility to act. Kant may have gone about things in the wrong way when he tried to establish the existence of God as a postulate needed for the moral life, but he was not wrong in relating moral agency to the issue of the divine.[1] Of course the Christian sense of God is not simply the phenomenon of divinity that appears to human agents, but unless the natural condition of agency is made clear, the special Christian sense cannot be theologically brought out. For this reason we now turn to Aristotle's treatment of virtue, vice, and action.

Kantian moral philosophy hinges on the distinction between passion and rational obligation, between inclination and moral imperatives. For Kant the human agent is established in the contrast and the conflict between these two parts of the human being. Aristotle works with a similar distinction, but he interprets it differently. He distinguishes between reason and the part of the human being that can be habituated to behave in a certain pattern, but he observes that such human inclinations, once habituated, need not be in conflict with reason. Instead Aristotle distinguishes four formal possibilities for human character: an agent may be virtuous, or self-controlled, or weak in self-control, or vicious. These are the four points of orientation for identifying moral character, the four different ways of being an agent. In addition there are two forms that are off the scale of normal human agency: being godlike and being brutish. To distinguish these kinds of human agents is of utmost importance in understanding Aristotle's *Nicomachean Ethics*; commentators and translators frequently go wrong because the various kinds are confused with one another. But of still greater importance is the fact that this array of distinctions is indispensable in bringing out the nature of human action, and it is strategic in contrasting natural with theological virtues.[2]

(1) A virtuous man is one in whom both reason and habituated inclination are disposed to do what is right: to act courageously and not rashly or cowardly when danger or hardship must be faced; to be generous and not avaricious or profligate; to do what is just and not to seek selfishly his own advantage. (2) A self-controlled man is one whose reason is in accord with what is right, but whose inclinations are in conflict with reason. He does not exist in the harmony found in the virtuous man; he requires self-control. Since he possesses self-control, he generally masters his inclinations and usually does what is good, but not without the need to master himself. The Greek term for self-control is *enkrateia* and the self-controlled agent is called *enkratēs*; the terms are often translated "continence" and "continent." Sometimes this state of character is equated with temperance, but such an equation is misleading, since temperance is the harmonious, virtuous state; and self-control, although good, is not the same as virtue. (3) A person weak in self-control is also one whose inclinations are in conflict with reason, but he is not able to master his inclinations. His reason is disposed correctly but it is often overcome by inclination; this kind of man, Aristotle observes, often repents for what he does (VII 8, 1150b30−31). He is persuaded to do what is right, but he often cannot do it. The Greek term for weakness in self-control is *akrasia* and the man so disposed is called *akratēs*; the terms are often translated "incontinence" and "incontinent." Sometimes this state of character is equated with intemperance or self-indulgence, but such an equation is wrong; self-indulgence is a vice; it is not weakness. (4) Finally, a vicious man is one whose mind and inclinations both move toward what is bad. He does not have to struggle with himself,

nor is he overcome by inclination, against his better judgment, as the weak person is. He chooses what is wrong and consequently is not likely to repent (VII 7, 1150a21; 8, 1150b29 – 30).

It is most important to leave these four states of character intact and not to reduce any one to another. Virtue and self-control are to be kept distinct; and yet, because they belong to the same genus, they are related and they clarify one another (VII 1, 1145a35 – b2). We understand one only in contrast to the other. Likewise vice and weakness in self-control must be kept distinct even though they too belong to a single genus and illuminate each other. We can therefore be good either by being virtuous or by being self-controlled, and we can be bad either through weakness or through vice; the good and the bad in human affairs are analogous terms, and moral phenomena are dangerously obfuscated if these analogies are not kept alive.[3]

Still another pair of moral kinds that Aristotle mentions are the godlike and the brutish. The brutish (*thēriōdēs*) is that which simply fails to be a human agent: through savagery, disease, or corruption one is simply not there as an agent in whom reason plays a role (VII 1, 5). This state is "beyond the limits of vice" (VII 5, 1148b34 – 1149a1), because in vice there is choice and mind. The brutish is something that should be human but either has ceased to be or has never become so. The brutish may well be fearsome, or an object of curiosity, or simply pathetic, but it does not have the power to appraise and act; it is outside both vice and weakness. Aristotle even says the brutish is of a different genus than vice (VII 1, 1145a27). At the other extreme there is what Aristotle calls the godlike: "virtue beyond us (*huper hēmas*), heroic and divine" (VII 1, 1145a19 – 20). Because of Machiavellian and Nietzschean influences we tend to think of this kind of agent as somehow beyond good and evil, but Aristotle does not mean to say that this heroic type does any kind of actions that the virtuous man would not do. The difference is that the godlike man has his goodness somewhat independently of the community which brought him up, while the virtuous man is good thanks to both his born disposition and his upbringing. The godlike or heroic man is given by nature as a way of bringing about virtue in

men. Although most virtue and self-control are there by guidance and training, there would be no beginning of virtue if
some exceptions did not occur to show what the possibilities of
action are. Locke is true to Aristotle when he describes this
kind of person in these terms: "I confess, there are some men's
constitutions of body and mind so vigorous, and well framed by
nature, that they need not much assistance from others, but by
the strength of their natural genius, they are from their cradles
carried towards what is excellent; and by the privilege of their
happy constitutions, are able to do wonders." He is also very
Aristotelian in the remark that follows: "But examples of this
kind are but few, and I think I may say, that of all the men we
meet with, nine parts of ten are what they are, good or evil,
useful or not, by their education."[4] Because of the origins of his
goodness, the heroic agent may possess his virtue more completely and more intensely than even the virtuous man possesses his, so the godlike man is said to have "an excess of
virtue," and his state is said to be "more honorable than virtue"
(VII 1, 1145a23 – 27). But although his goodness is "beyond us"
and beyond the civility and conventions that normally establish
virtue, he is not somehow "liberated," as the biases of modernity might make us think, to act apart from what is good by
nature. This would be nonsensical for Aristotle. Heroic virtue
and cultivated virtue both bring out what is good according to
nature. That is what makes them good.

For our purposes we may leave out further consideration of
the godlike and the brutish extremes and concentrate on the
four types of moral agents that make up the normal spectrum
of human conduct. To recognize these four is important for the
correct understanding of Aristotle's moral philosophy. Self-
control and weakness are extensively treated only in Book VII
of the *Nicomachean Ethics,* after having been introduced in Book I,
chapter thirteen, and mentioned sporadically after that. Until
Book VII, therefore, Aristotle is really discussing virtue or the
virtuous man. Most people, Aristotle observes, fall between
self-control and weakness (VII 7, 1150a15 – 16), so virtue is rare
in human affairs, but its rarity does not diminish its ethical
significance. The analyses found in Books I – VI work out the

structures and elements of virtuous action as the point around which other moral phenomena find their orientation; this theoretic relation to virtue corresponds to what occurs in actual human practice, where human conduct acquires its tone, stability, and direction from the example of virtuous men.

The four kinds of agents — virtuous, self-controlled, weak, and vicious — are somewhat formal kinds, like the four points of the compass or the basic colors of the spectrum. In actuality, agents will be placed at all stages of the continuum that stretches through these kinds, but the agents can be identified by their relation to the pure kind. Furthermore, these four kinds represent permanent states of character; they are not temporary conditions we move in and out of. A person weak in self-control is weak generally, not now and then; a temperate person is temperate steadily, not on occasion; a self-indulgent or greedy person is reliably self-indulgent or greedy. These are stable ways of acting, and we expect people to act according to character in the future, once they have become old enough to have a character. It is true that a virtuous person may, for example, on occasion perform an act which might be called uncontrolled, but this is *pathos* and not *ēthos*, an episode of passion and not character, and we often look for special reasons or excuses to explain the event; it requires explanation, whereas actions done according to character do not.[5] There can be shifts this way or that among these kinds: a person who is self-controlled may become weak or a weak person may acquire control or even move toward virtue, but such changes in direction are exceptional, take a very long time, and usually require much conduct modulating the agent toward the new state. Moral momentum is not easy to redirect. Finally, the four kinds of agency are not shown to us through introspective self-analysis. They are names for different kinds of people. They are distinguished, not by a reflective study of one's felt experience, but by an examination of how people behave. They are part of a public ontology of action. They illuminate how we can exist as agents; they do not tell us what the structure of our moral experience is.

Other distinctions that Aristotle makes in regard to action

are related to the various kinds of character in moral agency. For example, his claim that virtuous action is constituted as a middle between two possible extremes implies that the agent is able to know what conduct would be a middle between the two possibilities of failure. Not everyone knows how to act well in a situation calling for action, how to act and yet to avoid the extremes of rashness and timidity when danger has to be faced, how to be generous without being either prodigal or stingy. The middle always emerges as contrasted to the two possibilities of failure (and not as contrasted to a single opposite), and the middle can be more or less accurately hit; changing circumstances always mean that no automatic rule can determine for us what the appropriate action is; therefore our good judgment, our prudence, must come into play, and our character will affect our ability to strike the right conduct. A virtuous person will have a sense of the middle, while a self-controlled agent may need more help in determining what to do, and a weak person may be even less perceptive. A vicious person may simply choose one of the extremes, like the cowardly or the greedy action. In fact, a person who is deficient in virtue may not even realize that a particular situation calls for action; it takes some goodness to see that, say, generosity or temperance is called for.[6] Some people may pass by a situation without ever appreciating that something can and should be done in it, and whether they do the action or not depends on their character, on the kind of moral agents they have become.

And character, the origin of action, is established only by acting. It is the deposit of actions, first those done under the guidance and in the imitation of others, then those we become able to do on our own. Hearing speeches or reading books or knowing things theoretically does not provide the ability to act and to exercise prudence. Only conduct leads to the possibility of further conduct. This is true not only in the life of a single person but also in the moral development of a community. The stories and moral maxims that become part of moral education themselves stem from actions. We do not first figure out intellectually what ought to be done; good action originates in actual exercise and then becomes established in words. Thinking and prudence are involved in such action, but they are not the application of principles or knowledge that is somehow acquired before agency. Even what is good by nature is first disclosed in action; only thereafter is it more abstractly formulated. That self-indulgence is wrong by nature is not read off a theoretical pattern of the human essence but is disclosed in the exercise of human conduct, and the involvement of temperate people is required for it to be disclosed: they must be able to exemplify the good action and its contrast with its corresponding vices, and they must be able to say something about the goodness of what they do. Moral theory has its roots and principles in conduct.

The moral philosophy we inherit from Kant and from other sources, and the general opinions people now tend to have about morals, do not take their bearings from the four kinds of moral agency described by Aristotle (the virtuous, the self-controlled, the weak, and the vicious). Thought about morals tends to confine itself to the two middle kinds. It is assumed that there always is conflict between inclination and moral knowledge or the moral law, and ethical experience is evaluated in terms of how the conflict is resolved. The moral good is almost always seen as an obligation, as something that is binding and imposed. It is interpreted as alien to us, alien to how we would normally behave. The possibility of its being so much a part of an agent that the agent himself becomes the standard of what should be done is not admitted and certainly not exploited in moral understanding; the possibility of virtuous character, of harmony between moral reason and inclination, is not factored into what we say about morals. In fact, the very experience of conflict between obligation and inclination seems to be required for authentic moral behavior; only a person who has to master himself seems deserving of moral approval. The one who is virtuous and in harmony with himself seems to have too easy a time of it to deserve any merit. The self-controlled person, or even the weak person who, struggling away, just might manage to do what is right, seems to be the paragon of moral goodness.

This constriction of morals to the issue of self-control internalizes moral phenomena. Since we assume everyone is structured the same way, with passion opposed to reason, there is no need to identify, publicly and in open behavior, different kinds of character. The moral issue becomes the internal experience of conflict and the resolution of such conflict. Moral experience is internalized so much in Kant that he denies that we can ever identify a good action by seeing the public act itself; what makes an action good is, not something publicly visible, but the internal disposition of a good will, which never shows up as a moral phenomenon. The act as such is not praised or condemned; it is the will to do it out of duty and not out of inclination that deserves approbation, and this will is not a part of the public performance. The substance of the action is not publicly displayed: "For when moral worth is in question, it is not a matter of actions which one sees, but of their inner principles which one does not see."[7] For Aristotle, in contrast, the praiseworthiness of an agent's action is as visible, analogously, as is the skill of a craftsman or an athlete. We show what kind of agent we are in the actions we perform and in the choices we make.

The concentration of moral theory on self-control instead of virtue forces the separation of moral reason from inclination. In consequence, the thought arises that we ought to be able to map out our obligations by some sort of clear reasoning, so that we will know the "values" or "rules" according to which our passions should be directed. We are tempted to look for criteria or methods of reasoning that will generate our obligations for us before we act. We think it might be possible for us abstractly to recognize what is right. If such speculation does not succeed in generating obligations that everyone can agree upon, we may despair of moral reasoning and say all morals are simply customs. Or instead of looking to abstract reasoning, we may turn to moral facts, to the way people actually behave, and try to generalize what we discover there; but then what we reach is devoid of any sense of a moral obligation. We seem to have only moral facts, not values; or we have values just as facts. Such divagations in moral theory, between emphasizing the abstract value and turning to moral facts, occur because the ballast and direction provided by the virtuous agent is overlooked. The virtuous agent shows the excellence that is possible in human behavior, just as a superior athlete shows what can be done in a particular game. Virtuous behavior shows how human nature is capable of acting, and it shows thereby what human nature is, since the nature of a thing is most truly displayed when the thing is working at its best. A good agent has to take circumstances into account, but what he does settles into a normative generality; he becomes an example of what can and ought to be done "in similar circumstances." And since there are basic similarities in human situations, it is possible to get guidance from general norms that arise from the accumulation of human experience. The virtuous act is therefore both a fact and a value. When the general maxims for conduct have to be incorporated into a situation calling for action, however, prudence or moral perception is always needed to know which combination of issues is at stake and how the inevitable conflict among goods and obligations is to be resolved. Here again virtue is necessary to know what to do; an action is almost never identified simply by subsuming a case under a clear rule for conduct. And if virtue provides a better ability to perceive what should be done, and greater confidence even in being flexible to fit the act to the situation, self-control and weakness in self-control will tend to look more to the external authority, to the rigid rule, precisely because they cannot rely on their own prudence.

If the constriction of moral theory to forms of self-control makes us neglect the virtuous agent, it also makes us lose sight of vice as a human possibility. In vice both inclination and thinking are directed to what is bad. The vicious agent chooses self-indulgence, chooses to avoid danger when danger should be faced and is not ashamed to do so, chooses avarice or miserliness, chooses to defraud or to exploit others. A person weak in self-control may behave, say, self-indulgently but he does so against what he thinks he should do. To some extent he is overcome, or lapses out of action, and he is the kind of person who, sadly, is often moved instead of being the mover. But the vicious man is aware of what he is doing and wants to do it. He is an agent and a bad one. He might even be very smart in understanding a situation and seeing what can be done in it: Aristotle says a man can be clever without being prudent, because prudence involves a virtuous character, while cleverness is just the ability to map out relationships between means and ends (VI 12, 1144a23 – b4). The name used for the clever man is *deinos*, an adjective which in Greek has also the sense of the fearful and the terrible; as Gadamer has observed, it is as though the phenomenon of intelligence without virtue but in the service of vice, the spectacle of someone with brain power but without moral sensibility, were a dreadful and sorry sight in human affairs.[8]

But the emphasis on self-control makes us think that all agents really want to be good, and if they do something wrong, even if they do so habitually, it must deep down be, we suppose, against their better judgment. We tend to interpret vice as extreme weakness in self-control, extreme *akrasia*. The strong momentum of character and habit is overlooked, and the need to educate character may as a consequence be neglected. Because vice is not seen as a possibility in human action, we may not guard against it, and the theoretical confusion about moral possibilities may have damaging practical consequences in moral education and public policy. Like virtue, vice is not common, normally, in human life; most people tend toward the middle of the possibilities of human conduct. But vice can occur, and under some circumstances it can proliferate. It is certainly easier for people to fall into vice than to rise to virtue. And although our earlier remarks about the virtuous man may make it sound as if he executed his good deeds with effortless grace, the fact is that there is hardly ever a human situation in which virtue does not have to assert itself against the pressures of vice or weakness. Virtue is virtue because there is always not only the possibility but the insistence of vice. This struggle occurs publicly among people; it is not primarily a conflict in the secrecy of our hearts. The well-ordered soul is not experienced introspectively and not discovered through reflection on the motives that lie behind what we do; it becomes visible in public action, just as the disordered soul does. Our moral state is the

source of our conduct and shows up in how we behave. It is
not what we internally feel.

Human action occurs within what Hannah Arendt has called
the web of human relationships.[9] Action continually establishes
and adjusts these relationships. We are there for one another as
agents who have acted for others and have had others act for
us. We emerge more or less distinctly as figures in these relationships and as qualified in this way or that, according as we
have acted. For example, if someone has been defrauded by
someone else, he has not just lost something; he is henceforth
there as one who has been defrauded by another. He is even
henceforth there for himself as one who has been defrauded by
another. If someone has been courageous, he is there as one
who was courageous for those who needed his courage. A person's reputation and the gossip that attends him are simply an
echo, persistent, sometimes accurate and sometimes not, of
what he has done. If something merely happens in and through
us, through accident or illness or compulsion, we are not there
as agents, and others are not newly related to us by what has
occurred; we must be the beginning of the act if the web is to
be constricted, relaxed, broken, slightly unravelled, or modified
in tone by us. And everyone has done something, but some are
more agents than others: weakness in self-control, for example,
is a kind of submergence into natural forces; hence Aristotle
says we must turn to those who study natural science, to the
"physiologists" (and not to the rhetoricians), to find what can
be done for it (VII 3, 1147b6 – 9; 1147a10 – 25). Such lassitude
is not the same as the vice of indolence. And finally among
those who do act there are those who act well and those who
act viciously.

The ability to emerge as an agent requires the ability to
think about the situation that calls for something to be done.
Such thinking is not the consideration of maxims and the placing of a case under a general rule; it is more elementary, more
of a raw articulation of what is really going on. It is an appraisal of a concrete situation. It involves generalities, but the
focus of the thought is not on the general but on the situation.
It is a recognition that something should be done, and it is a

projection of what can be done. In the immediacy of a situation such thinking lets ends emerge and unravels arrays of means. It exhibits insight into what is at issue and shows imagination about what can be done. It requires maturity and prudence to be able to shake out ends and means, to see a difference between what we do right now and what we are trying ultimately to get done. Impetuosity, for example, cannot make this distinction between means and ends. To illuminate our situation as one calling for action is an understanding, and as an understanding it is necessarily our own.[10] Since the thinking and appraisal are necessarily our own, our character enters into and is displayed by the understanding we achieve. Even to be able to conceive of doing certain things is an indication of what kind of person one is. A virtuous person will be able to exercise such intelligence and to achieve such thinking better than someone who is not virtuous, but even a good man will need friends to help appraise the possibilities of conduct in particularly serious situations (III 3, 1112b10–11; VIII 1, 1155a16). There may be some situations that a virtuous man can understand but that a self-controlled person, precisely because of the heteronomy of his goodness, cannot handle. And there may arise many other situations that simply permit no possibilities of action, no matter how virtuous or resourceful the persons involved in them may be; they call simply for resignation, not practical understanding.

In the course of life we are — unless the spring of affection has been broken — constantly appraising our situation, appraising it more or less thoughtfully, and constantly showing who and what we are. What we are can be affected by many things that happen to us; but it is determined by what we have done and by what others have done for us.

NOTES

1. *Critique of Practical Reason*, Part I, Book II, chapter 2, section 5.
2. The distinction between virtue and self-control, and its impor-

tance for interpreting Aristotle and for treating ethical issues in themselves, was shown to me by Francis Slade. For a bibliographical note concerning this topic see Appendix I.

3. On some details concerning virtue and self-control in Aristotle's text see Appendix I.

4. *Some Thoughts concerning Education*, §1, in *The Educational Writings of John Locke*, edited by James L. Axtell (Cambridge: Cambridge University Press, 1968), p. 114.

5. Samuel Johnson's friends believed of him "That though he might be charged with bad humor at times, he was always a good-natured man." James Boswell, *The Life of Samuel Johnson* (New York: Random House, n.d.), p. 368.

6. See the remarkable essay by W.W. Fortenbaugh, "Aristotle's Conception of Moral Virtue and Its Perceptive Role," *American Philological Association, Transactions and Proceedings* 95 (1964): 77 – 87.

7. *Foundations of the Metaphysics of Morals*, translated by Lewis White Beck (Indianapolis: Bobbs-Merrill, 1959), p. 23.

8. Hans-Georg Gadamer, *Wahrheit und Methode* (Tubingen: Siebeck, 1965), pp. 306 – 7.

9. Hannah Arendt, *The Human Condition* (Chicago: The University of Chicago Press, 1958), p. 183.

10. See Michael Oakeshott, *On Human Conduct* (Oxford: Clarendon, 1975), p. 37.

7. Theological Virtue

Human action, as it is described by Aristotle and other pagan philosophers, occurs within the setting bordered by the world and its necessities. Human affairs emerge within nature, and in convention and *technē* they become distinguished from that which is simply by nature. In being so distinguished they allow the natural to appear as such. Action is disclosed on its own terms when philosophy begins to distinguish nature, convention, and craft, and when it begins to think about being as it differentiates itself in these forms. The terms appropriate to action are elaborated when philosophy differentiates itself from myth and displays the differences between nature, convention, and *technē* that are either unnoticed or obliterated in myth. But although action is distinguished from nature, it is still placed within a world which is greater than action and which gives an orientation for action. This is vividly stated by Aristotle, who insists that man is not the best thing in the cosmos and that the regular, irresistible movement of the heavens provides a steady background for the fluctuating affairs of men. And although men actualize themselves as men through their actions, their thinking can reach beyond human affairs: when we think, we touch on being as that which is present in the necessary as well as the contingent, in the natural as well as the human. Thinking can even become indifferent to human affairs, because it is concerned with nature, the world, and being, which range beyond the human.

This setting for human action is changed when the world is seen as created and God is appreciated as creator. The steady

anonymity of the world, in and against which action occurs, is
now seen as the effect of a choice, and the unforced generosity
behind that choice is seen as what most truly exists. Human
action, correspondingly, is now obligated in a new way: it must
not only bring itself forward in virtue in order to become itself;
it must also respond to the generosity of creation and to the
still greater generosity of the incarnation and redemption. This
can be a disorienting demand. It is difficult enough to involve
the necessities of the world into virtue and self-control; such
necessities are at least regular and the good in them is adapt-
able to the human scale. But the apparent excess of generosity
and the extreme goodness and independence of the God who
does not need to create leave us practically at a loss as to what
we ought to do and how we are to do it. Even natural virtue
cannot act appropriately in this context, and our confidence as
human agents is disturbed. It is perhaps at this point more than
any other that the relationship between faith and reason, between grace and nature, must be correctly lived and and com-
prehended, because the introduction of the new setting in faith,
if badly understood, may make us think that confidence in action must be replaced by timidity or foolhardiness, that prudence must be replaced by indecision, that nobility must yield
to obsequiousness: in sum, that natural virtue must give
way to an associated vice or to weakness of will. To suppose
such things would indicate that the relationship between what is
by nature and what is by grace has not been correctly understood. What is good by nature remains good in the setting in
which grace is required; its goodness is in fact enhanced, not
distorted, by the new context.

But in order to discuss the integrity of what is and remains
good by nature, we must first bring out more fully the differences between the natural and the Christian. The differences
are made vivid, for example, in the interpretation of human
vice and wickedness. No one is more aware than Aristotle of
the presence of malice. He not only states that man is not the
best thing in the world; he also says, "For man, when perfected, is the best of all animals, but when separated from law
and justice, he is the worst of all." He goes on, "If he does not

have virtue, he is the most unholy and the most savage of animals, and the most full of lust and gluttony" (Politics I 2, 1253a31 – 38). The human ability to identify and differentiate, when cultivated, becomes reason, law, and justice; but uncultivated it makes man capable of behavior worse than that of any beast. Aristotle also observes that most men avoid bad actions not through shame but through fear, that they live by passion, pursue their own pleasures, and hardly recognize the noble and the truly pleasant (Nicomachean Ethics X 9, 1179a33 – b20). Therefore, he says, laws are needed as a kind of reason to make up for the virtue and reason lacking in so many people. This sour picture of the human condition is presented by Aristotole as the way things simply are and the way they always will be. The only way of dealing with the human tendency to wickedness is to cultivate virtue and to bring about law and justice; the effort to do so will be required as long as there are human beings.

Within Christian belief, however, the obvious reality of wickedness is interpreted as something that need not have been. It is so interpreted, not because Christianity has had different experiences of people than the pagan philosophers have had, but because of the understanding of God achieved in Christianity. If God is as he is believed to be, then wickedness cannot simply be part of the way things have to be. The presence of wickedness and the inclination to badness could not have been brought about by the infinitely good creator, so they must be there out of some sort of failure or out of something like a choice made by the creature; the name for this failure or choice is original sin. And the bad actions that people perform are not just seen as blameworthy, punishable, shameful, disgusting, or even unholy. They are now seen as sins: not because they display a perceptible feature they did not show before, but because the same actions are now seen within the setting of creation. Bad people do not merely act against what they are, against their human nature. Because this nature is seen to be created and not simply part of how things are, such agents act against their creator: they do not merely act badly and unlawfully; they also sin. But when bad actions are seen as sins, it does not change the truth that the way to struggle against vice and against the inclination to badness is to cultivate virtue and to bring about law and justice.

Even the interpretation of human wickedness as something we can be redeemed from occurs together with the proclamation of salvation through Christ, and against the background of creation, with its questioning of the ultimacy of evil. Aristotle, Plato, and other pagan thinkers did not expect man to be released from the invariable tendency to fall toward vice and weakness; the tendency was simply there as the necessity within which virtue and reason had to do the best they could. Furthermore, the rejection of salvation — as it occurred during the life of Christ and as it continues in the history of Christianity — can also be seen as a rejection of salvation only when human wickedness is appreciated within the context of creation and redemption. It is not simply cruelty or selfishness or pride, but the mystery of sin that is expressed in the prologue to St. John's Gospel: "He was in the world, and the world was made through him, and the world knew him not."

Wickedness becomes interpreted as sin within the Christian understanding; but what is to count as virtue in the new setting that Christian belief provides for human being? It is one thing to try to imitate the courage or justice of good men; no matter how rare, such virtues remain on the human scale. But what is to be done before the generosity of the creator, and how are we to respond to the incarnation, the crucifixion, and the resurrection? We are supposed to act in a setting not limited by the necessities of the world. In fact, our involvement in this new setting is cultivated in what have been called the theological virtues of faith, hope, and charity. These are not simply new virtues to be added to what Aristotle, Plato, or the Stoics described as the excellences of human being. They are specifically the dispositions for "acting" in the setting disclosed by Christian faith; they are the source of the "reaction" we are to have to the God who creates without any need for creation and who involves us in his own life through his Son. And strictly speaking we simply cannot act on our own in this new setting. Our natural place for acting, the scene we ourselves can manage to some extent through virtue, law, and reason, is the world of human affairs bounded by the impenetrable necessities of the cosmos. There we are on our own. But the beginning, the continuation, and the success of our life of responding to God are all a gift of grace.

For example, natural virtue is acquired by doing good actions, first under the guidance of others and then on our own. Once someone becomes virtuous, he can rely on his own character and can take pride in himself. But no actions of ours, no matter how virtuous or generous, can bring about our life with God. If we exercise faith, hope, and charity, the very exercise is a gift from God. We do not have the resources to enter into this life: not because we are failures as human beings, but because no created and finite being can involve itself with the life led by God. It would be an incoherence to think a creature could do so on its own. The exercise and confirmation of the theological virtues obviously involves prayer, sharing faith and hope with others, acts of generosity, asceticism, and so on, but these "actions" serve to "cultivate" the theological virtues in a way different from the way naturally good actions establish and strengthen natural virtue. The full story of what happens in Christian action is not the visible generosity or patience or courage; the action has a dimension that remains hidden in a way analogous to the way the divinity of Christ was hidden during his life on earth, and for the same reason: what is being done is, not merely an action within the setting of the world and its necessities, but an involvement with God who is not a part of the world. And yet this other dimension in human action, this working of grace, is identifiable with the acts done by the human agent. The substance of what a Christian does in faith, hope, and charity is not simply the human action, but it is identifiable with the human action. The differences within which such identifications take place are articulated when the world is taken no longer as the final setting for action, but as the place in which God the creator has intervened to make available his own divine life.

Furthermore, once a person becomes temperate or generous or courageous, both that person and other people know that he is temperate or generous or courageous; he keeps acting that way and can be relied upon to act that way in the future. But the theological virtues do not appear in the same public way. As St. Thomas says, we may have signs that indicate that we are living in grace before God (he mentions as examples that a person may perceive that he delights in God, spurns mundane things, and is aware of no mortal sin), but experiencing such signs is not a perception of the possession of grace; and the reason we cannot perceive directly that we live in grace is that "the principle of grace, and its object, is God himself, who is unknown to us because of his excellence" (*Summa theologiae* I II q. 112, art. 5). Supernatural virtue is not available as a mundane phenomenon, as natural virtue is. Scotus says something similar: "By natural reason nothing supernatural can be shown to exist in the wayfarer, nor can it be proved that anything supernatural is necessarily required for his perfection. Neither can one who has something supernatural know it is in him."[1] Of course we can appreciate that a person is a good and even a holy Christian, but his faith, hope, and charity are not manifest in the same way that moral virtue is manifest, and it is not verifiable in the way moral virtue can be verified.

The life of grace, as something to be established, lived, and perhaps lost, has, in its unperceivability, an unsettling effect on the natural moral life. We can no longer rest confident in our virtue; natural virtue does not provide salvation. Because it does not save us, we may be tempted to disparage natural virtue, call it pride, and claim that even the weak and the despised, if they live in grace, are "better" than the virtuous. But such a claim involves a confusion of two kinds of virtue, the natural and the theological, and it attempts to substitute the theological for the natural. Or we may go to the other extreme and demand a natural evidence for theological virtue: we may want a feeling of being saved or a perception of grace so that we will have an assurance for the life of grace somehow similar to the assurances we have in the moral life. We try to interpret theological virtue according to the form of experience of natural virtue. In both such cases the confusion and the false expectation result from a failure to differentiate the new Christian setting for action from the setting for human action provided by the world.

The difference between the two contexts can be brought out more sharply if we make use of the kinds of natural human character we distinguished in the previous chapter: the virtuous, the self-controlled, the weak, and the vicious. Because the theological virtues of faith, hope, and charity are never achieved by our own efforts but come to us through the actions of Christ and from God's mercy, they seem to fall more appropriately into the categories of self-control and weakness in self-control; they seem to involve a law over and against our inclinations, a law that demands a permanent struggle for self-mastery. It would be a kind of incoherent arrogance to claim that we can incorporate grace and the theological virtues so thoroughly into our character that we exist in theological virtue on our own, the way Aristotle's virtuous man lives in his courage, temperance, and justice. Among human beings, it seems, only Christ is theologically the fully virtuous man; all the rest seem to depend on an outside source and measure for their virtue. And at the other extreme, it seems that the solidity and permanence of vice as Aristotle describes it are shaken by the possibility of conversion that is open to everyone. It seems that no one could be fixed in vice as a permanent state of character, because even the worst sinner can be forgiven. Virtue and vice seem therefore to recede as permanent moral states, and it appears that the most appropriate way of describing human moral behavior, when it is seen against the background of grace, is in terms of strength and weakness in self-control. Thus the Christian teaching on the theological virtues, along with influences from Stoicism and from social and political developments in human life, helped move moral theory to concentrate its attention on self-control as the primary moral phenomenon, and helped draw its attention away from the virtuous and the vicious agents as points of orientation for ethics.

But the two settings for action and the two kinds of virtue must be distinguished. The stability of character that natural virtue provides and the example and measure that it furnishes continue within the context of grace. Natural virtue does not

achieve grace, but it remains natural virtue. It is not turned into
self-control or weakness. Likewise, weakness in self-control is
not turned into natural virtue if the person who is weak begins
to live in Christian faith. He remains a person who has to
struggle against inclinations that frequently win out over his
better judgment; this condition remains unless he moves
toward mastery over his inclinations, but he can achieve such
mastery only by acting in a self-controlled way and by letting
the new direction of his actions settle into his character. Grace
as such does not make him actually different in respect to the
categories of virtue, vice, and self-control. This contrast of the
two kinds of virtue, the natural and the theological, is often the
theme of literary treatments of Christianity. Very often such
works will describe someone who is weak in self-control,
someone say who cannot master the inclination to alcohol or to
sensuality, but who struggles with these inclinations and in this
struggle still serves as an example of faith, hope, and charity.
The very paradox of combining weakness with theological virtue in the same agent is a literary device that writers could not
possibly resist, especially writers who live within the axioms of
modernity.

The truth in this paradox is the theological truth that God's
work is not achieved through human virtue and that God can
choose even the weak to make his grace manifest. But this
shows that God's grace is of an order different from human
excellence; and if it is wrong to make grace depend on human
achievement, it is equally confused and confusing to let grace
turn virtue into vice, arrogance, or hypocrisy, and to deprive
the well-ordered soul of its strength and exemplarity. Grace
and the theological virtues do not obliterate the distinction between virtue, vice, and self-mastery, and they do not destroy
the fact that virtuous action emerges as a middle between two
possible ways of failing, by excess and by defect, and that this
course of action may be more excellently achieved the more
virtuous the agent is. They do not circumvent the need for the
actual performance of actions as the only way to establish
character, and they do not eliminate the need for prudence, for
practical reason, in knowing what should be done when a situ-

ation calls for action. The determinations of natural virtue remain what they are. Grace and the theological virtues must be so understood that natural virtue and the essentials of the moral life retain their integrity when involved with Christian action, and they can be so understood only in the contrast of the two final settings for action: the setting of the world and its necessities as the place for human action and its excellence, and the setting of Christian belief, in which the world is seen as existing through generosity and God is appreciated as the one who could be all that there is, with no diminution of goodness or greatness. The theological virtues are what enable us to "act" in this Christian setting, in the light of a generosity that has no measure in the virtues and excellences of natural behavior.

The complexity in the relationship between natural and theological virtues is brought out in the analysis St. Thomas makes of them. He distinguishes between the natural virtues, which stem from possibilities in human nature and which are brought to perfection by exercise, and what he calls the "infused" virtues. The theological virtues of faith, hope, and charity need to be infused in us by God (*Summa theologiae* I II q. 63, art. 1– 2), but along with charity, Aquinas says, "all the moral virtues are infused" (I II q. 65, art. 2; q. 63, art. 3). That is, there are a whole series of infused, supernatural moral virtues that we possess through grace: infused fortitude, infused temperance, infused prudence. These infused virtues are different "in species" from the natural moral virtues that we cultivate by our own actions, because the infused moral virtues make us capable of acting in respect to our life with God, while the natural ones make us fit to act in human affairs; and because the behavior we are urged to perform by the infused virtues will differ from that urged by the natural ones: natural temperance, for example, moderates our use of food and drink in view of health and the exercise of reason, but infused virtue will urge us toward asceticism (I II q. 63, art. 4). So we seem to have not only a contrast between moral and theological virtues but also a contrast between two levels of moral virtue, the natural and the infused. In what sense does one remain a single

agent in such differences? And how are the infused moral virtues to be compared with the acquired moral virtues? For
example, could a person who is weak in self-control as regards
natural virtue be, at the same time, temperate and courageous
through his infused virtue? Does he acquire such temperance
and courage simply by infusion, without actual performance?
Aquinas has things to say about these questions, and we will
study his remarks presently, but as a first impression, we seem
to be faced with something like two characters, two origins of
action in a single agent, the one acquired and the other infused.

But after duplicating the source of action by speaking of two
distinct kinds of virtue, Aquinas goes still further: he says that
"only the infused virtues are perfect, and are to be called virtues *simpliciter*. . . . The other virtues, the acquired ones, are
virtues *secundum quid*, but not *simpliciter*" (I II q. 65, art. 2). After
having distinguished sharply between natural and infused moral
virtues, he claims that natural virtues, those that we normally
experience, those that provide the stability and guidance for
human life, those that are the first kind of virtue that we
encounter and name as virtues, that such natural virtues are
virtues only "in a way" and not in the primary sense. The
reason for this is that the infused virtues enable man to act
toward his true and final end, while the others enable him to
act toward an end which is final only in one restricted area, in
one genus, the genus of civic life. Aquinas says that virtue is
analogous and that the primary sense is found in infused virtue,
while the secondary, derived sense is found in natural moral
virtue, which conditions us "only" for civic life and human
affairs. Aristotle also considers "good action" to be analogous,
but he says that the primary sense of human goodness is found
in the virtuous man, while the derived form is found in self-
control. But when Aquinas positions natural virtue against the
context of the Christian life, what seemed to be the most real
moral excellence takes on the coloration of virtue in a secondary, derived sense.

Yet Aquinas does not stop with this shift in the primary
sense of virtue; he goes on to quote the statement from Romans 14:23, "For all that is not from faith is sin," and he

mentions Augustine's gloss, "Where there is no recognition of the truth, virtue is false, even in good habits" (I II q. 65, art. 2). Aquinas seems not only to move natural virtue to second place; in quoting Augustine he seems to say that noninfused, acquired virtue only appears to be virtue but really is not: it is "false virtue." How can false virtue be virtue even *secundum quid*? How can it be virtue at all? And earlier in the same article Aquinas admitted that acquired virtues can exist, albeit without charity, in many pagans. So he seems to concede the true existence of natural virtues without grace. And yet, from the point of view of the final end of man, good dispositions that fail to serve the final end do somehow seem to be bleached of their goodness. How is this to be understood? What meaning do the terms "false" and "true" have when they are used this way in regard to virtue? Such questions are raised, not to make Aquinas's doctrine on the virtues look confused, but to bring out more fully the problems, the *aporiae*, that theological reflection must face when it examines human "actions" within the Christian setting. Theologically it must be made clear what perspective one is speaking from when one is able to say, when one must say, that acquired human virtues are "false" virtues.

Natural moral virtue is thus made to shift from being the best in man, to being the best in a derived sense, to being, apparently, only a false "best." But there are still other shifts in the meaning of virtue between Aristotle and Aquinas. The way in which virtue is a habit is changed. For Aristotle virtue is a firm, established way of acting. It is the result of many actions that settle into a character (*ēthos*) and into habits (*hexeis*). Aristotle says explicitly that virtues are not either passions or powers (*dunameis; Nicomachean Ethics* II 5, 1106a6–13). Aquinas also claims that virtues, both acquired and infused, are habits, but he expands the sense of habit so that it takes on some of the features of an ability, a disposition to be able to act, something like what Aristotle would call a power. Aquinas admits that perfect virtues and habits are those that result from many actions, but he also speaks of the initial ability to perform as a habit or virtue. This is done most conspicuously in regard to the infused moral and theological virtues. A child who is baptized, for example, would possess the infused virtues and habits, both theological and moral, even though they are not yet perfected and not yet even exercised, because the child has become able to act in the life of grace. Instead of being the culmination and the deposit of actions, virtue and habit are the original beginning of performance. Aquinas makes use of the category of habit to explain how we are made able to "act" in the supernatural context; we must receive these habits and virtues to be able to do anything at all, so they cannot be the result of our earlier performances. But in this theological adaptation the sense of habit and virtue is changed. The feature of being acquired by performance is muted.

Aquinas admits that someone who receives the infused moral virtues may still experience difficulty in acting according to them because of "impediments coming in from outside (*extrinsecus*)," obstacles that come from "contrary dispositions remaining from earlier actions" (I II q. 65, art. 3 ad 2). He compares this conflict to the obstacles we might experience in exercising our understanding when we are impeded by drowsiness or by illness; he thus uses the example of an intellectual virtue to shed light on this moral conflict. His description of conflict between what we should do and what we are disposed to do sounds very much like the description Aristotle gives of the self-controlled man. Furthermore, Aquinas realizes that such a conflict will not arise in the case of natural virtue: "This difficulty [in performance] does not occur in the same way in the acquired moral virtues: because the contrary dispositions are removed through the exercise of the acts by which such virtues are acquired." Thus someone can have the habit of infused moral virtue without yet having the facility and delight in performance that virtue in the natural sense provides. In addition, Aquinas says that the infused moral virtues, which come to the believer with charity, are lost if charity is lost through mortal sin (I II q. 65, art. 3). Here the infused moral virtues seem to be deprived of the permanence and reliability that virtuous character has in Aristotle, since charity can be lost even by a single action which is a deliberate and serious turning away from God (*De caritate*, art. 13). Virtue and habit take on a

very different tone when they are displaced from natural behavior to the setting of grace.

Even in the treatment of natural, acquired virtue there is a
difference of interpretation between Aristotle and Aquinas. For
Aristotle virtue is found in those men whose inclinations are in
harmony with reason, and the virtuous man is contrasted to the
self-controlled, the weak, and the vicious. Virtue is located in
one special kind of agent. But for Aquinas virtue is present in
almost all agents, who realize it in different degrees. Aquinas
frequently mentions the "beginnings" of virtue, the *inchoationes
virtutum* or the *inchoatio virtutis*, as something that all men possess simply by being men (*De virtutibus in communi*, art. 8; *Summa
theologiae* I II q. 63, art. 1). He admits that some individuals are
more inclined by nature to virtue than others are. He acknowledges that full and perfect virtue is acquired only when our
abilities to act become habituated to act well, but he sees
human nature as inclined from the start toward these good
states. Instead of the fourfold array given by Aristotle, Aquinas
presents us with a continuum stretching from the beginning of
virtue through the gradually more perfect achievements of it. In
this scheme the contrast between virtue and self-control is
dimmed. The noble seems almost to be changed into the
obligatory. Aquinas differs from Aristotle because he understands men as created and as inclined by the creator toward
goodness; there is a kind of "effective" teleology in Aquinas'
understanding of man that must be distinguished from Aristotelian entelechies and teleologies, which are not seen in the
context of creation and do not regulate the development of a
being in the same way as do those described by Aquinas. The
four kinds of character are in Aristotle four possible consolida-
tions of human agency, but in Aquinas the various kinds of
agents, the better and the worse, are seen as developments or
frustrations of a single inclination of man toward his proper
end.

In all these ways the concepts of action and virtue are modified in the new setting for human existence, which is disclosed
in Christian faith. Many theoretical problems arise from these
modifications, especially if the new concepts of virtue and ac-

tion are separated from their Christian theological context and
used in what is proposed as a direct description of natural
moral phenomena. Both the theological and the philosophical
understanding suffer in such a transposition, and it becomes
difficult to see moral phenomena on their own terms. This is
the situation we are in now. Modern ethical theory shows the
effect of Christian theology even when it is carried out independently of Christian faith. And the danger of ambiguity and
confusion is compounded even more for theology as it attempts
to find its voice and to differentiate itself from an ethical theory
that is theologically influenced; it is like trying to distinguish a
voice from its own echo.

But before discussing, in the next chapter, how we can now
speak theologically about human action, one further topic must
be examined. We have drawn a sharp distinction between virtue
as it is naturally experienced and virtue as it is theologically
believed. Following Aquinas, we have even distinguished between acquired moral virtues and infused moral virtues. We
may have given the impression that the single human agent is
split into two performers when the two contexts of action, the
natural and the theological, are introduced, and that the single
agent is supposed to do two very different kinds of things:
some related to simply being human and others related to the
life of grace. But when we turn from a rather abstract formulation of this double agency to a more concrete study of what
exactly the person is supposed to do, we find a much greater
unity in action. The obligation or the possibility of doing what
is good by nature unifies what might, in the abstract, seem to
be two different performances. In the concrete situation, when
something should be done, what the Christian is primarily supposed to do is what the good man would be expected to do: to
tell the truth, to be honest, to be temperate and courageous, to
care for one's family, to defend one's home and country, and
the like. The sketches of virtuous action provided by Aristotle
in Books III-V of the *Nicomachean Ethics* can and must be appropriated in a description of what someone who is both virtuous and a Christian would be expected to do; the *bonum hones-
tum*, that which is noble and good, remains that which should

be done by the Christian agent. The possibilities of acting well that a Christian sees are such that they should be visible as good to anyone who is a good person himself. What is good by nature is a kind of ballast for Christian action; when one appraises a situation from the Christian viewpoint, what one sees as to be done is primarily what should be done if one is to act according to human nature and according to the natures of the things involved in the action. The Christian perspective does not bring in obligations that are at odds with what we ought to do according to the nature of things; the Christian illumination of what is to be done consists first of all in confirming what is good by nature, and in appreciating that what is good according to nature is not simply good in itself but also good because created and therefore willed by God. What is good by nature is not set over against what is good by grace but is integrated into it. And what is good by grace is not simply a matter of convention and arbitrary decision; rather it builds on nature and shares in the reasonableness associated with nature.

It is true that Christian belief may emphasize certain aspects of natural moral goods. Because of its belief in creation and redemption, Christian moral doctrine will draw attention to the sameness of all human beings as created and loved and redeemed by God, and this emphasis should make Christians more attentive to the needs and dignity of the weak, the unborn, and the poor, whose humanity may be less impressive than that of people who have made conspicuous achievements in life. But to draw attention to the fact that all men are men and deserve some recognition as men is not to import something totally unheard-of in natural moral understanding. Even in issues that are controversial in the wider society, such as the issues of abortion and infanticide, the Christian moral understanding is put forward, not simply as a religious belief or a sectarian opinion, but as a position that can be argued as morally right according to nature. Even the more specifically religious and Christian forms of moral behavior, such as the community life of religious societies, the vows of poverty, chastity, and obedience, the practice of prayer and asceticism, and the works of corporeal and spiritual charity, all exploit possibilities of human moral virtue and are recognizable as good — even if their full sense may not be appreciated — by persons who are morally sensitive in a natural way. All such actions may and should acquire a specifically Christian tone, but they are not in conflict with what is naturally good; on the contrary, in practice they both bring out and are stabilized by natural virtue and prudence.

Furthermore, although Christian belief may emphasize the common dignity of all men as created and loved by God, it does not reduce to insignificance the many differences that exist among them, nor does it imply that all people should be treated exactly alike: there remain differences between the good and the bad, between the talented and the untalented, the strong and the weak, leaders and followers, and friends and strangers, and such differences must be taken into account when we act, even though they are seen against a setting in which the common humanity of all men is made more vivid. Christian belief does not diminish, for example, the public honor that is due to virtue, and it obviously does not imply that public responsibility should be given to the ignorant or the incompetent instead of to those who are suited for it. Such discriminations are not eliminated when Christians emphasize the common dignity of all men before God. And of course the decision as to how all these factors are to be brought together in a virtuous course of action depends ineluctably on the prudence, on the power of appraisal, of virtuous agents; no scheme, formula, or pattern can ever take the place of such persons in determining concretely what ought to be done.

In this context the Christian virtue of humility and the Christian practice of penitence call perhaps for special comment. Christian belief discloses a setting in which a human being understands himself as created by God and as called to a life in which his own talents and efforts cannot be sufficient. His realistic appraisal of his own worth and ability is modified by this belief; a Christian has a sense of gratitude and adoration toward the creator that a pagan will not have, for no matter how much a pagan may reverence the divine, he stands somewhat on his own over against the gods: he is brought about by nature and by his parents and his society, but not by the choice of a creator. And whatever he accomplishes, despite all the help given by others, is somehow radically his own. The context of creation introduces a dimension in which a person's being his own is itself seen as a gift, and the belief in redemption and grace introduces a domain of behavior, one of ultimate importance, in which what is to be done can only be accomplished in dependence on Christ and in union with him. In this setting of creation and grace a kind of humility is appropriate which is not proper to natural life and natural virtue, but this humility does not compete with the confidence and pride that mark natural virtue and natural ability, and it does not make the believer insecure in his actions as a human being. Once again, prudence and good judgment are required to integrate the natural and the graced, and the example of persons who live the combination of natural pride and supernatural humility is the best argument that the two can be lived together as one.

To someone who does not understand Christian belief the practice of penitence may appear to be either an obsession with guilt where no explicit fault has been committed or a behavior that is pointless because it tries to work against something that will be there no matter what we do about it, the tendency of people to fall into wickedness. The unbeliever might find repentance appropriate for bad acts one has oneself committed, but he may well question the value of doing penance for the wickedness of others or for the malice of men in general. Why, for example, should the Carmelites lead a cloistered and penitential life in the convent at the prison site at Dachau? What good does it do? The motive for the virtue of penitence is, of course, not a theoretical statement but the example of Christ. Through his words and actions Christ has brought us to understand that the state of malice and wickedness, which in the Christian perspective is seen to be sin, is not purely and simply the way things had to be; and through his death and resurrection Christ has made a life without sin available to man. He achieved this through suffering. Why it had to be done this way is not clear to us, although it does seem clear that a redemption that did not involve suffering and death would have left something undone and something in us untouched. Suffering and sin seem in some way to be related to each other (although suffering and wickedness do not seem to be so connected); sin seems to bring about suffering, and suffering seems to have the power to release us from sin.

Christian penitence is not simply temperance, not just abstinence, and not merely a kind of reparation for one's own misdeeds; it is an attempt to join with Christ in the suffering of his redemptive actions. It is neither morbid nor a sullen denial of things that are good and pleasant; it is an attempt to affirm goodness, in union with Christ, even in the isolation that pain and hardship bring when they come upon us. It is an attempt to face sin and suffering and still to assert the goodness of God. The specifically Christian relationships of Christ with all men, and of all men with one another as children of God, are required to make sense of the virtue of penitence. We may not be able to comprehend positively why and how suffering can release us and others from sin, no more than we can clearly and positively see why Christ had to suffer and die to bring about our redemption; but we can appreciate that a life without repentance and penitence simply turns aside from the issue of sin and fails to "act" in regard to sin.

Suffering and the kind of guilt that occurs beyond law do not belong to those things that can be understood by reason or determined by our own initiatives. Such guilt and suffering are mysterious even within the setting of reason and nature. Perhaps the closest Aristotle comes to treating them is in the *Poetics*. In a dramatic performance the tragic event that we know can occur to any one of us is depicted and externalized before us. Although we may not be able to "do" anything about such a thing, we are able to live through it at a distance and, to some extent, in another; and in this concrete and individual way we may be able to comprehend it in its expressive form, even though we could never understand it in its causes and nature and reasonableness, because as a tragic event and as suffering it does not enjoy causes, does not have a nature, and is opaque to reason. Even in Aristotle such tragedy is associated with a fault, *hamartia*, in the way things are, but this fault is not seen as a sin against the creator. Within Christian belief one can accept suffering, and even assume deprivation and hardship, for one's own redemption from sin and for that of others; this possibility exists because of the redemption brought about by Christ and because we can join our actions with his. The redemptive death of Christ is not just a spectacle for us but an event in which we can take part. But when we take part in it, we find no objective measure of justice prescribed, no amount of rectification that can be agreed upon as an adequate penitence and reparation; we deal with things that are beyond the law. The discernment of what is fitting, considering both the natural and the theological, is done, not through a calculation of equivalences, but through prudence formed by religious sensibility, holiness, and the experience of the church.

NOTE

1. John Duns Scotus, "On The Necessity of Revealed Knowledge" (Prologue of the *Ordinatio* of John Duns Scotus), §12, translated by Allan Wolter, O.F.M., *Franciscan Studies* 11 (1951): 244.

8. The Theology of Disclosure

Augustine has said, and Aquinas has quoted him as saying, that natural virtue without faith is false virtue. We might well be uncomfortable with this assertion. It seems to deny what is obvious. According to every natural measure there were and there are good, prudent men among those who do not share the Christian faith. Furthermore, the center of what Christians believe, God as the creator and as independent of the world, does not appear as one of the natural phenomena in the world. This understanding of God, with all its mystery, is used to assert that what looks, sounds, and feels like virtue is "really" false virtue. What can falsity mean here? Moreover, if the natural virtues turn out to be false virtues, where does that leave the infused virtues, whether theological or moral, since the supernatural virtues are defined as virtues in contrast to the natural? The infused virtues seem left without a foil.

The reason for these dilemmas is found the special new context within which the infused virtues are supposed to permit the believer to act. The theological context is not simply another human setting or another possibility within the world. If it were, it would be easy to explain how the partial virtue was truncated and hence false in its own kind. For example, one can understood how familial loyalties that take no account of civic obligations can be distorted and hence false as loyalties: nepotism is not true allegiance to one's family; it only looks like it to some people. It is, in an obvious sense, false as a virtue. However, there is no behavior to be found in natural human affairs that can intrude in this way to show the falsity of natural virtue as a whole; natural moral excellence is supposed to encompass the whole of human action, not merely one part of it, so there is no room left for another part to appear and render what is achieved in natural virtue limited and illusory. The way the supernatural virtues and the context for their actions intrude on natural activity is not the way a further kind of natural activity would intervene, so the sense of "falsity" at issue here is not the sense one normally uses in discrediting human behavior.[1]

An instinct that it is not fair to natural virtue to call it false has caused theological reflection to recoil to the other extreme and to see the theological virtues as a kind of fulfillment of what is anticipated in natural moral activity. Human nature is said to be inclined from the beginning toward the activities it achieves in faith, hope, and charity. The distinction between the natural and the supernatural is deemphasized; the Christian message is said to be that which everyone is more or less waiting for, at least obscurely, and the power of human thought and desire to transcend any particular object is taken as an anticipation of Christian revelation, of the Christian understanding of God, and of the Christian questioning of the world as a whole. In some cases this theological position may consider the various cultural forms in which human transcendence is expressed, the different philosophies and religions, as practically equivalent to Christian belief and as equally successful fulfillments of human nature; in other cases it may present Christianity as the best and most complete form of what the other religions, philosophies, and artistic endeavors achieve in a less perfect way. From the fact, which we believe through faith, that the creator has involved man in the divine life, it is inferred that man anticipates, at least vaguely, his involvement in the life of God and that signs of this anticipation can be deciphered not only in various religious and cultural phenomena but even in the development of an individual person, who is said to move from a response to the love of his parents, his friends, and his society, toward a response to the love of the God who created and redeemed him, and that he moves through all these stages in a continuous progression.

This interpretation of the natural and the supernatural would not tend to call the natural virtues false, but it has other inconveniences. The special character of Christian belief is not emphasized; Christianity appears as simply a development, even if the highest development, of human transcendence and the religious instinct. Revelation and grace appear as something due to human nature. What we might call the density of the simply natural, the fact that it has its own kind of wholeness on its own kind of terms, is neglected; the non-Christian is too quickly deciphered into an anticipation or an approximation or an equivalent of the Christian. The Christian setting, with its belief in the creator and the world as created, is taken as the first, obvious, and natural setting for human existence and for the exercise of reason.

Both these extremes seem inadequate: to dismiss natural virtue as false and to consider natural virtue as simply identifiable with what is done through grace. But how is theological thinking to come to terms with the distinction between what is by nature and what is by grace? It is not enough to continue inspecting the two terms of the distinction, the natural and the graced, in an effort to find what is common and what is different in them. It is necessary to move to different ground and to pay attention to the distinction itself, not just to its terms. Instead of comparing the theological good with the natural, it is necessary to examine how the one comes to light against the other, to show how the theological good becomes differentiated from the natural good.

To do this we must distinguish three ways in which the Christian good and the natural good are approached.

(1) From within what we might call simple faith, natural virtues and goods are presented and acquired together with what is believed and practiced in faith. Moderation, courage, honesty, and other virtues are taught simply as parts of what one does as a good Christian, along with the practices of faith, hope, and charity, and with the sacraments, prayers, and religious devotions. Natural virtues are motivated by Christian as well as human considerations; it is the creator's will that a person exercise moderation, and an imitation of Christ will

include truthfulness and courage. Many of the virtues St. Paul exhorts Christians to practice are simple human virtues: for example, he says the lazy, meddling brothers at Thessalonica either should get work or should not be allowed to eat.[2] In this direct living of the faith all the virtues are simply practiced together. It may even be felt that a loss of faith might threaten all the virtues one has acquired. Likewise, the life that one led before accepting the faith — if one was not raised in the faith from the beginning — may be interpreted as somehow deficient in true virtue.[3] This simple, direct living of both the natural virtues and the faith, this bundling of the two, is naive, but not in any pejorative sense of the term. It is the way one grows into the faith and the unified way one lives in it. The direct life of faith is what one returns to after all the theoretical distinctions have been made, and the theoretical distinctions are made in order to let this life be lived in its directness and simplicity.

(2) Now instead of simply acting in response to the Christian message, we can begin to think about God as the good for which we act and live. Let us call this reflection the "theology of Christian things." In carrying it out we must contrast the Christian good, and the context of action in which it is situated, with the human good we know from moral experience. We realize that moral activity is common to all men but Christian faith is not. Helped by the reflections on the moral good made by those who do not share Christian belief, we reflect both on natural moral experience and on the actions done in faith. We thus have before us two goods, two final "things," the natural and the Christian. Our reflection is done within the setting established by faith, and in this setting the natural human good appears derivative and partial.

It is within this sort of theoretical reflection, this theology of Christian things, that we seem to be faced with the uncomfortable alternative of either calling the natural virtues false or somehow equating the natural and the infused virtues. Neither alternative seems adequate, but we cannot resolve the dilemma by bringing forth new reasons that will show that one or the other of the two choices is after all the right one; or by denying that this is the alternative we are faced with; or indeed by trying to reformulate the meaning of either the theological good or the natural moral good in such a way as to escape this choice. Rather, the theological move that we must make is a turn to a new kind of consideration.

(3) In this new dimension of theological thinking we try to determine how the theological good comes to light; or, perhaps more accurately, we try to determine how the theological good becomes light. We try to show how the distinction between the natural and the Christian good occurs. We think about how God is presented or disclosed as the one toward whom our faith, hope, and charity are turned. Such thinking can be called the "theology of disclosure," in contrast to the theology of Christian things or Christian realities that we have just examined. Of course we remain concerned with Christian things, but we now turn our attention to the way in which they become manifest. We are now concerned with their being distinguished from the things we live with in the world. We must undertake such thinking about disclosure if we are to say anything about truth and falsity; even in natural experience we must discuss manifestation if we are to clarify what we mean by the true and the false. Therefore if we wish to clarify what is meant theologically when natural virtue without faith is said to be false virtue, we must leave the theology of things and turn to the theology of disclosure.

The theology of disclosure deals with the way Christian realities come forward, but it also deals with the way they are distinguished. It deals with the Christian distinction itself. Distinction and manifestation are here treated together, and indeed they belong together, because for something to become manifest is for it to be distinguished. The theology of disclosure is engaged, not in two enterprises when it studies manifestation and distinction, but only in one. The theology of things, however, deals, not with the Christian distinction as such, but with the terms of the distinction, with God and the world, or perhaps with God and man; the theology of things takes the distinction for granted.

It is possible to register necessities in the manifestation of Christian things. There are necessities not only in things but also in the way things must appear. It might seem that such a study would deal "only" with the human way of knowing things, that it is "only" an anthropology or an epistemology. The disclosure might seem to be separable from the things disclosed. But this is not the case. If we can bring out necessities in the way things must appear, we thereby say something about the being of such things. If things must be presented or absented in certain ways, if they demand to be distinguished from certain other things, it is because they exist in a certain way. It is not happpenstance that the Christian realities emerge by differentiation from natural things. The theology of disclosure and the theology of Christian things must therefore be developed in tandem.

After these rather abstract remarks about things and disclosure it will be helpful to illustrate how the two theologies, of things and of disclosure, reinforce one another. A first example can be found in the theological problem of evil. In Christian faith we believe that God has created the world. When this belief is articulated by the theology of Christian things, we are given a formal statement of how beings and events have been derived: God creates the world and sustains it in existence, there is a choice made by some creatures against the will of God, this sinful choice pervades the world of human affairs, but man and the world are redeemed by God's mercy as expressed in the incarnation, death, and resurrection of his Son, and the world now awaits a final restoration in God. This pattern of emanation and return is found in many theological writings and is the framework for the *Summa theologiae* of St. Thomas. In elaborating this descent and return a theologian will work out many details, such as the character of sin and of original sin, the theology of the Trinity, the question of human freedom and the divine law, and so on. Such studies present the way theological things are "in themselves." But there seems to be something missing in this kind of analysis. The choice against God's will, for example, seems to come out of nowhere. Sin seems almost to betray a deficiency in creation. Also, after this analysis is made, it seems somewhat disconnected from both the lived faith and the biblical narration which are its source. It

seems almost accidental to these things that they should also be
made manifest to people in the accounts given in the scriptures
and in the disclosure proper to faith. Somehow a greater involvement of the appearance of such things seems to be called
for.

But if one were to think about the disclosure of Christian
things, one would not start by saying that wickedness and suffering were there out of a choice against God's will. One would
first see them with their own necessity and ineluctability, as
Aristotle and other philosophers saw them. They just are the
way things are. Then, theologically, one would bring out the
sense of redemption from evil. Wickedness and suffering are
then seen to be involved with sin, and they become understood
as not having had to be there at all; they become understood as
not coming from the all-good creator. The priority of God's
goodness is now asserted in contrast to what first appears as an
inevitable presence of evils. The natural ultimacy and necessity
of wickedness and suffering are made to be a foil against which
the Christian sense of the divine is brought out, and a new
context is introduced in which the ultimacy and necessity of
wickedness and suffering are questioned. The Christian things,
those things discussed by the "ontological" theology we described earlier, are reached again, but they are reached by the
insertion of a contrast with natural necessities.

At this point, however, we do not just move into the theology of things and leave the issue of disclosure behind. The
theology of disclosure is not merely an entrance into the theology of things. The issue of disclosure is kept alive, and the
primary, natural necessity of malice and suffering, the sense
that natural experience gives us that such things somehow
simply have to be, is not allowed to vanish. It is continually
played off against what one comes to in the theology of Christian things. When we get to what is first in itself, we do not
dismiss what is first for us; by keeping alive what is first for us,
we appreciate more truly what it means for the Christian things
to be first in themselves.

To take evil and suffering as not absolutely final, to see them
as a result of choice and not of necessity, to see them as some-

thing from which we can be redeemed, is part of the good news of Christianity. But when we understand the Christian "nonnecessity" of evil and suffering by holding it in contrast to the necessity that evil and suffering have for natural experience, we are less inclined to raise some of the awkward problems that surface when we remain simply with the theology of things. We are less tempted to ask questions like Why did God ever permit evil and suffering? Or, Could God not have prevented sin? Or, Why did God afflict this person with such a tragedy? It is not that we now have answers to such questions, but we do appreciate more vividly that they are inappropriate questions. The important thing is that evil and suffering, which seem so dense and so dark, somehow did not have to be, that God is not subordinated to them, and that we can be saved from them. Questions about why God permits evil, or why he permitted a particular evil to befall us, begin to look like idle questions when we appreciate the impact of the truth that evil is not a last word. And we can appreciate this impact more fully in the interplay of the theology of disclosure and the theology of things.

A second example of the relationship between these two theologies concerns the issue of human subordination. Aristotle claims that men are subordinated to one another not only by convention but also by nature. In describing those who are subordinate by nature Aristotle says that it is better for such people to have their lives ordered by someone else because they themselves do not have foresight and are not able to initiate action.[4] Their own well-being depends on the guidance of others. For Aristotle this distinction between the naturally superior and the naturally inferior is a "last thing" that we come to when we analyze human affairs; it is not a result of something, it is not emendable, and it is not a transformation of any sort of equality that is more basic and more real than the subordination. In St. Augustine, however, we find it said that human beings were created equal by God, who "did not wish a rational creature, made in his own image, to have dominion save over irrational creatures: not man over man, but man over the beasts." Augustine says that "the first just men

were established as shepherds of flocks, rather than as kings of
men." He says that slavery arose when "those who by the law
of war might have been put to death, when preserved by their
victors, became slaves" and that both wars and slavery were
the consequences of sin. He continues, "By nature, in which
God first created man, no man is the slave either of another
man or of sin," and he looks forward to a condition in which
"all wickedness [will] pass away and all lordship and human
authority be done away with and God be all in all" (The City of
God XIX 15). Augustine thus looks through the unequal condition of men, that condition which is opaque to Aristotle, and
says that because they are created in the image of God, men
are all equal. The density of human subordination gives way to
equality. Aquinas holds a partly different doctrine; he says that
servile subordination, "by virtue of which a superior makes use
of a subject for his own benefit," was introduced after sin, but
that familial and civic subordination existed among men even
before there was sin.[5]

According to these Christian thinkers the subordination
found among men, at least in its servile form, stands in need of
explanation. It is not a natural and fundamental phenomenon.
We can think beyond it to a condition of equality from which
the inequality can be derived. Later political philosophers, like
Hobbes, Locke, and Rousseau, also stressed the natural equality
of men and thought it necessary to explain the origins of ser-
vitude; and like Augustine they even thought it necessary to
explain how the subordination in political society came about.
Their emphasis on the social contract also reflects a belief that
all men are essentially equal and able to enter into a contract;
Hobbes even says that a slave makes a special kind of contract
with his master. Modern liberal democracies continue to assert
the equality of all men, and modern social and economic conditions may serve to deemphasize the differences that would
surface if men acted more immediately upon one another. But
the original insistence on human equality was related to Christian belief in the creation of man. When we carry out the
theology of Christian things, we may assert equality as the basic
condition of men, but if we turn to the theology of disclosure,

we would have to show how this sense of equality differentiates itself from the natural subordination described by Aristotle.

There are other examples of how the interplay of things and disclosure can illuminate issues that arise in Christian belief. The accidental can be allowed to remain accidental in the natural order, for instance, and yet be accepted as the will of God; conversion, or *metanoia*, can be shown not to signify instability of character; confidence in God's providence can be shown not to diminish the need for prudence and initiative. We can appreciate somewhat more adequately why miracles do not compel belief, why Christ did not appear to everyone after his resurrection, why petitionary prayer is good even if it is not answered in the way we desire. The sense in which salvation frees us from law can be appreciated only if the full strength and necessity of the law is acknowledged and God's mercy is held in contrast with it. Many perplexing issues arise because we somehow feel that we ought to be able to understand Christian things simply as they are in themselves, as though the point of view which presents only that which is first in itself were the only point of view there is. We become more moderate in the kind of explanation we want when we see such issues at the intersection of the theology of disclosure and the theology of things; we do get a sense of why things have to be the way they are in Christian belief. If we blend these two theologies, we keep alive the differentiation of the Christian setting from the world or the whole, and we remain sensitive to the transformation of language, the move into analogy, that is at the core of Christian thinking.

The theology of disclosure is, of course, not just a report of how this person or that happens to feel about the Christian faith, or how this person or that happens to experience the things of the faith. The theology of disclosure examines how the things of the faith must be presented; it attempts to state essential distinctions that must occur in the emergence of what Christians believe. It tries to show how Christian things are differentiated from things experienced in nature. Such theological thinking may well seem to be "closer to life" than the analysis of Christian things, since we live our lives in the way things appear. But in the way things appear we also have presenced to us the way things are in themselves; in fact our great desire should be to live according to the way things are in themselves and to take care that we do not impede them from seeming to us as they truly are.

It is not only possible for us to carry out theological reflection on the disclosure of Christian faith; it is also appropriate to develop theology in this way at this particular time. The issue of appearances has been crucial in philosophy since the late Middle Ages. During this era the way of being of appearances has been improperly understood. Appearances have been interpreted as merely subjective or psychological and have been separated philosophically from the things that appear in them. This misunderstanding of appearances has not been merely a minor inconvenience in philosophy and in modern culture. It has confused our thought about being, about the good, about human action, and about human existence itself; it has radically distorted our appreciation of truth. There are many political, economic, religious, and philosophical reasons why appearances have been treated in this way, and there have been political, economic, religious, and philosophical repercussions of such treatment.

But because of philosophical developments in this century it is now possible to speak more coherently and more appropriately about appearances, about the dative for appearing, and about the things disclosed in the process of appearance. It is possible to speak about such matters in a more wholesome and less fragmenting way than in the past. Such discourse can and should be exploited in Christian theology, not simply to make theology up-to-date but in order to come to terms with issues that have been germinating in theological inquiry without being able to find their proper formulation. Such a study of appearances, of presences and absences, may make it possible for us to find more to appropriate in the neoplatonic form of theology found in the fathers of the church. We may be able to take more seriously the various emanations, concealments, identities, and illuminations that might have seemed to us to be quaint and metaphorical rather than true. But this new focus is not a simple return to the fathers, because it appreciates itself as subsequent to the style and the achievements of scholasticism and it incorporates what scholastic theology, with its exploration of Christian things, has done. It is not like the patristic return one finds in Newman, who assimilated the fathers without allowing scholastic thinking to have an effect on his mind. But the study of disclosure is not a simple return to scholastic thinking either, because it takes advantage of the modern focus on appearances and attempts to bring out structures in manifestation that may not have been visible before.

Another reason why a theological analysis of disclosure is appropriate at this time is that it can acknowledge the necessity of history in Christian faith, and it can do so without being reduced to historicism. If a distinction is to be made and an appearance is to occur, the distinction must be made somewhere and at some time, even though what is distinguished and manifested need not be reduced to what happens in that place at that time. To know all about the circumstances, languages, and personalities involved in achieving a distinction may shed some light on the distinction itself and on the things that are manifest in it. It is helpful and important to learn about these historical matters, but the historical materials acquire their significance because of their involvement in the distinction and the terms distinguished. We do not busy ourselves with them merely as historical curiosities. And it is also true that the distinction and the terms distinguished can be made available and kept alive even if some of the historical information concerning the circumstances of their origins is incomplete or unavailable. The faith did not begin only when critical history arrived on the scene.

We can now return to the issue that was raised at the beginning of this chapter: the question of why theology seems forced to oscillate between the two extremes of either holding natural virtue to be false virtue or seeing in natural virtue the anticipation or the equivalent of infused virtue. This question prompted us to make explicit the distinction between a theology directed toward the things believed in Christian faith and a theology that reflects on the way such things are disclosed. We

have not only distinguished these two functions of theology but
have insisted that they belong together and that some necessities can be appreciated precisely in the interaction of one with
the other. The question of natural and infused virtue is clarified
by positioning these theologies against each other.

Natural virtue is what we begin with in human experience.
Theological virtue is disclosed in contrast with it, so theological
virtue cannot say that natural virtue does not exist or that it is
simply false. However, the disclosure of the theological is so
special, and the kind of activity it opens for human beings is so
different, that natural virtue does not render us capable in any
way of behaving in the new context. Hence natural virtue
comes to light as not able any longer to let us act: from this
perspective it changes its color and is "not" virtue. But the
"not" and the "false" are severely transformed when they are
used in this context, and they do not suggest the sort of denial
or unreality that occurs in natural human affairs. The theological exploration of this issue would demand many particular
distinctions, contrasts, and refinements, many moves that lance
ambiguities and dispel confusions; it gets its force by being
worked out in detail, not simply by being stated in principle.
But the point of principle we must emphasize is that to leave
by itself the simple and bald statement that natural virtue is
false virtue, to leave this remark, which is made in the theology
of things, as simply the last word is theologically incomplete.
The appropriate "truth" and "falsity" of natural virtue has to
be stated in the study of the disclosure of virtue in the two
contexts, the natural and the theological. Without this further
theological clarification we do not know what "falsity" means
when it is used theologically.

From our analysis of how theological realities come forward,
we can also appreciate how one would be inclined to see
theological virtue as simply fulfilling the natural desire for happiness. We can appreciate how someone within Christian belief
would say that the faith provides what men look for in life.
However, being sensitive to the displacement of contexts, we
would also appreciate the discontinuity between what we naturally want and what can be possessed in faith; we would ap-

preciate that what grace provides is given not in the way it is anticipated by nature. We would know that the senses of anticipation and fulfillment need to be specified for this issue, since we deal here with differentiations and identifications not like those found in the world. Being sensitive to the way the contexts are positioned against one another would make it unlikely that we would simply say, for example, that the only true anthropology is a Christology or that the movement of transcendence in natural human experience finds its proper completion in the knowledge we have of God as creator and redeemer. The Christian message is "newer" than such statements would have us believe. Such statements arise when we flatten theological analysis into fewer dimensions than it should have, or if we do not have a proper sense of the relationship between manifestations and things.

The theology of disclosure, then, helps us see that the oscillation between calling natural virtue false and identifying it somehow with infused virtue is bound to occur if we remain simply in the theology of things. It helps us see that this unwelcome alternative is unavoidable. But it also provides us with the flexibility and the new dimensions we need to appreciate what words like "true," "false," and "the same" mean when we enter the Christian setting. We are no longer simply caught by the alternative. The theology of disclosure makes an issue of the shift in contexts that occurs in Christian faith.

In our naive, direct living of Christian belief the presence of God in the world is emphasized. We stress that God is omnipresent as creator and that he has entered into our world as our redeemer. Theological reflection, especially the theology of disclosure, seems to dampen the enthusiasm of immediate belief because it emphasizes the ways in which God is not present. But this is not done to diminish the fervor of belief; it is done to bring out the differences that are required for the special kind of identification and presence that faith asserts. The theology of disclosure preserves the distinctive character of Christian belief. It prevents us from equating the presence of God with other kinds of mundane presences, whether those of worldly substances or those of things like the Platonic One. In this prevention it enhances our faith and allows it to stand out more vividly on its own terms. Thus the theology of disclosure can be related not only to the theology of things but also to the immediate life of Christian belief.

The blend of disclosure, things, and simple faith is illustrated in an oration of St. Anselm in which he praises the Blessed Virgin.[6] Anselm writes, "The sky, stars, earth, rivers, day and night . . . rejoice, our Lady." He says the presencing of such things had been distorted by idolatry: "For they were like dead things: they lost the dignity they were born with and for which they were made, of serving and helping those who praise God; and they were crushed and discolored by the use they were put to by those who serve idols, for whom they were not made." Thus it was not just things, but their presentation and their use that have gone awry. Sin in man has hindered them from truly being themselves. However, because of the consent of Mary, "They rejoice as if they had come to life again," and this occurs "because they are governed by the dominion and adorned by the use of those who believe in God." Our redemption restores not only the relationship between man and God but the way things are and the way they are presented to us: "God himself, who made all things, made himself from Mary. In this way he remade all that he had made." And God achieved this change in the "face" of things by waiting upon the response of the Virgin: "He who was able to make all things out of nothing, when they had been defaced would not remake them without first becoming Mary's son." Thus not just things but also the presentation and the use of things are restored from idolatry to true worship, and this action of God is made to depend on the response of the Virgin.

The earlier chapters of this book were an exercise in the theology of disclosure. Our discussion of creation, of the Christian understanding of God, and of the Christian sense of the world as created, was an attempt to differentiate the Christian setting from that of the world as a whole; to think about the differentiation is also to think about the terms disclosed in it and to think about how they are disclosed. Therefore the question of the relation between natural and infused virtue, between nature and grace, leads back to the theological issue of creation and to the contrast between God and the world. Nature and grace can be discussed only with terms and distinctions derived from the theology of creation.

NOTES

1. Can an analogy for the supernatural and the natural be found in the way intellectual virtues supplement the moral? Are moral virtues "false" in some sense if they are based on a theoretical error? Not really, because the moral domain has its own completeness in regard to the intellectual. Moral virtue must include prudence, so there is an appropriate exercise of mind in moral agency, but prudence is not speculation.

2. II Thessalonians 3:6 — 12; see also Ephesians 4:25 — 32.

3. Romans 6:17 — 22; Ephesians 2:1 — 4; 4:17 — 24; 5:8; Colossians 1:21.

4. *Politics* I 1, 1252a30 — 34; 4, 1254a7 — 8.

5. *Summa theologiae* I q. 92, art. 1, ad 2; see q. 96, art. 4. Aristotle considers both servile and familial subordination to be prepolitical forms of order, and he treats them in Book I of the *Politics*. Aquinas distinguishes servile and familial subordination by saying that the second was found in the state of innocence but not the first.

6. St. Anselm, *Oratio ad sanctam Mariam pro impetranda eius et Christi amorem. Oratio VII. Opera Omnia*, vol. 3, edited by Francis S. Schmitt, O.S.B. (Edinburgh: Nelson, 1946), pp. 20 — 22.

9. That Truly God Exists

The issue of grace and natural virtue has brought us back to the issue of creation. Our first discussion of creation was carried out by way of a commentary on parts of St. Anselm's *Proslogion*. St. Anselm uses a specifically Christian understanding of God in his argument, and by reflecting on his texts we were able to differentiate the Christian from the pagan senses of the divine. But Anselm does more than merely present the Christian understanding of God; he also argues that when God is understood as that than which nothing greater or better can be thought, he cannot be thought not to exist. What are we to say about Anselm's reasoning as an argument that God truly exists?

The argument works with the contrast between existing in the mind and existing in reality. The way this opposition is defined in Anselm is unfortunate. He writes so forcefully about things we understand as being "in the mind, *in intellectu*" and "in thought, *in cogitatione,*" and he so takes for granted this mental kind of existence ("*quid hoc planius?* what more obvious than this?"), that the special form of being which is enjoyed by ideas and by things in the mind is neglected.[1] Anselm's remarks played no small role in masking the special condition of presences and thoughts and in generating ambiguities in the language we use to speak about appearances. It became almost impossible to avoid taking an idea as a sort of thing in the mind, even though later thinkers tried to modify this assumption by considering the concept to be just an accident of the soul and by qualifying it in many ways. The idea becomes something like a sign or a picture or a reflection of an object, but always it is there as an entity, and the question arises how we are to get through this thing in the mind to the thing in reality. The preposition "in" in the phrase "in the mind" tends to be taken in its original spatial sense, and its transformed, metaphorical character is overlooked; and "the mind," being governed by that spatial preposition, is taken as a place or a container. The entire vocabulary for thinking, for presenting, and even for being, gets pushed out of joint; thus the way is prepared for taking perception as a representation instead of a presentation.

Anselm did not achieve all these consequences, and he was not the only historical cause for them, but the emphasis and tone he used in speaking about existence in the mind contributed to them, especially since the issue of the existence of God was an important topic in scholasticism and was frequently discussed in terms of the alternative between existing in the mind and existing in reality. The two domains became reinforced in their opposition to each other, and appearances and presentations tended to become relegated to the psychological instead of being treated as belonging to the being of things. It is interesting that Anselm's critic Gaunilo tried to edge away from speaking of an existence in the mind; he tried to speak just of "understanding what is said" and grasping "the meaning of the word which is heard."[2] But his remarks are insufficiently worked out, and they are mixed with the issue of thinking about things that do not exist; Anselm simply replies that if anything is in fact understood, it must exist in the understanding.

Instead of speaking about an idea of God existing in the mind, a better way of discussing our thought about God is to speak about how God, and implicitly also the world, are to be understood. The issue is not whether a particular idea exists or does not exist in our minds, but whether or not things can be so understood that a "that than which nothing greater can be thought" makes sense. Such an interpretation of things, as we have seen, is not merely a thought of a single existent, God; it also involves a way of understanding the world, the whole presented to our experience and thought. The issue is, therefore,

whether things are such that a distinction can be made between
the world and God, these terms being so taken that the world
does not bring about anything greater or better when it is
added to God. The "idea" of God lives in this contrast, with
the special features that the contrast has. The distinction and
the understanding come together. It is a more fundamental
matter to determine whether this distinction can be made than
it is to determine whether one of the terms of the distinction,
the term that names God, has an object to which it refers in
reality.

This is why Anselm's major step is to establish what we
mean by God; his actual argument that God exists seems rather
quick and obvious. It also seems somehow unconvincing, even
though it may be hard to point out any logical flaws in it. We
are uneasy with it for two reasons: the serious philosophical
and theological issue lies, not in the explicit argument for existence, but in the establishment of the terms used in the proof;
and the argument works within an alternative, between being in
the mind and being in reality, which is inadequate and unlucky,
no matter how self-evident it may seem to be. The issue of
"greater" and "better" is defined and examined within this alternative of being in the mind and being in reality; if something
exists in reality as well as in the mind, it must be thought to be
greater and better than that which is in the mind alone. But the
more fundamental question of how the "greater" and "better"
between God and the world are to be determined is left un-
examined and only implicitly defined.

If the deeper issue in Anselm is whether the Christian distinction between God and the world can be made, what are we
to say about the question of the existence of God? Is something
more than a distinction needed to show that God, as understood in this distinction, does exist? We must avoid facile answers to such questions. It may seem easy to reply that the
distinction could be only a conceptual or mental distinction,
something only "in the mind," and that we must go on somehow to show that the distinction is not only mental or conceptual but also real. But is this a proper response? Is this how
distinctions "in the mind" are related to distinctions "in

things"? The making of distinctions in any domain of thought, theological or natural, is related to being in what might seem an unusual way. There is a kind of warrant of existence when a distinction that can be understood is made.[3] When we make distinctions, we do not have to follow them up with a proof that the terms of the distinction exist. Each term of a distinction seems to be able to assert itself as real precisely because it excludes something else. These considerations do not immediately show that Anselm's proof is correct, but they should make us more flexible in thinking about what a proof of existence can mean in the case we are examining.

Furthermore, the Christian distinction between God and the world is not like the distinctions we ordinarily make, because our standard distinctions are made within the setting of the world. The world is precisely the whole within which thinking makes discriminations. But in our present case the world itself becomes a term in the distinction, a term that is not of equal weight with the other term, God, since God is not defined in his being as God by being distinguished from the world; even if there were no world, God would be all that he is in undiminished goodness and greatness. By thus shifting its terms Christian theology defines its object in such a way that the normal identities and differences and possibilities and impossibilities that work within the world do not apply as they apply to things in the world. Hence, while natural, pagan philosophy may not suffice to establish the sense of God found in Christianity, it also cannot reason against it, since the entire setting for discourse and argument is fundamentally changed.

Furthermore, in the Christian distinction we do not distinguish between two kinds of things, like "worlds" and "divinities," but between two "individuals." The world as a whole is this world; it is not one individual instance of the species "world." The very contrast between individual and species hardly makes sense in regard to the world. And that which is distinguished as the other to the world, the God who could be even if the world were not, is also just the one God. In this respect the Christian distinction is analogous to the distinction we gradually come to make between "me" and "the world."

But it is only analogous, because the Christian distinction works even more radically with pure "individuals"; there are many respects in which "I" must understand myself as being an instance of one kind of thing among many kinds in the world.

Granted all these special characteristics of the fundamental Christian distinction, must we say that the making of the distinction itself somehow establishes for us the existence of God? The issue can be further clarified by contrasting our interpretation of St. Anselm with some other approaches to the existence of God.

(A) Making the Christian distinction between God and the world is a more elementary activity than carrying out the traditional arguments for the existence of God. The "five ways" of St. Thomas, for example, assume that Aristotelian metaphysics has given way to the metaphysics of *esse* and that the *ipsum esse subsistens* has been introduced. The horizon within which the five ways work is not explicitly established by the five ways, although it may be suggested by them. But this setting is brought about by what is going on in Anselm's reasoning. Anselm's argument may not do what Aquinas' proofs achieve, but it may accomplish something else. His argument does not reason from effects to causes, but it brings out the domain within which the movement from effects to causes is to take place. When we begin Christian theology, we must shift our inquiry from looking for the highest and first causes in the world to looking for the cause of the world or the whole, and Anselm's discussion may be used to draw attention to this adjustment.

(B) But if Anselm's argument is not simply a reasoning from sensible effects to their causes, it is also not the kind of reasoning carried out by writers in the tradition called transcendental Thomism. These thinkers turn to the unrestricted human desire to know; they remark that this desire cannot be satisfied by anything in the world and that it can transcend the world as a whole. The mind always has a further question. This unrestricted interrogation of being, they claim, does not find its completion except in the knowledge of infinite being. The question of being, moreover, is brought to things by the intellect; it is not read off what we experience. And when we do philosophy according to the transcendental method, we must try to appreciate being by thinking about knowledge and the desire to know. For example, Bernard Lonergan states, "Being is completely intelligible," and his reason for saying this is "For being is the objective of the detached, disinterested, unrestricted desire to know."[4] Finally, Lonergan infers from the complete intelligibility of being to the affirmation that God exists.[5]

This form of arguing, found not only in Lonergan but also in Rahner and others, assumes the perspective in which the world is understood as created.[6] The world is taken as transparent to its creator and hence "completely intelligible," and human thinking is taken as desiring to have all questions answered. Human desire and inquiry are taken as transcending any limited good. But this is how human beings understand themselves when they exist in a Christian self-understanding, in which the world or the whole is seen against a good and a truth infinitely greater than itself. The transcendental method does not accept the pagan state of mind as a real possibility with a kind of closure and completeness and obscurity of its own. Consequently it does not see the need to contrast the Christian and the pagan senses of the whole. The desire for the infinite and the search for unrestricted intelligibility are said to be phenomena that appear when we simply examine the human condition. This approach does not give due recognition to what we have examined in pagan mythical and philosophical thinking: the simple acceptance of limitation (which may not even be seen as limitation to be transcended) and the acknowledgment of elements of rude unintelligibility that show up along with the reasonableness of things.

(C) Still another approach to the existence of God can be found in the interpretation of St. Anselm that has been given by Karl Barth.[7] Barth stresses the fact that Anselm reasons within the setting of faith and claims that Anselm receives the understanding he has of God, the "idea" of God, from faith: "Anselm did not regard his designation for God . . . as a constituent part of a universal human awareness of God, but as an article of faith" (pp. 76 – 77). He also says, "It is a question of the proof of faith by faith which was already established in itself without proof" (p. 170). But Barth goes on to say that Anselm's definition of God does not tell us what God is: "All that the formula says about this object is, as far as I can see, this one thing, this one negative: nothing greater than it can be imagined" (p. 75). Barth interprets this name of God as a prohibition which commands us not to try to think of anything greater or better than God: "It does not say that God is, nor what he is, but rather, in the form of a prohibition that man can understand, who he is" (p. 75). Through the formula we understand the prohibition, but we do not understand the nature of God. When someone is presented with this name of God, he is "by no means confronted by a mere word . . . but by a prohibition which certainly does not contain or express anything about the existence of God but which nonetheless by setting a definite limit on concepts of God, describes existence *in intellectu*" (p. 114).

The name of God we find in Anselm "expresses nothing about the nature of God but rather lays down a rule of thought which, if we follow it, enables us to endorse the statements about the Nature of God accepted in faith . . . as our own necessary thoughts" (p. 80). This name of God involves "an injunction which it brings to expression" (p. 108), and, on the basis of faith, it rules out any conception of God that would allow us to think of anything greater or better than him: "In the way of any thinker who has a hankering in this direction, the revealed Name of the Lord . . . stands as an effective deterrent" (p. 83). Barth is aware of the importance of creation in this understanding of God. He speaks of the relationship of creation as revealed and as providing the setting for the name of God: "In this relationship [of creation] which is actualized by virtue of God's revelation, as he thinks of God he knows that he is under this prohibition: he can conceive of nothing greater, to be precise, 'better,' beyond God without lapsing into the absurdity, excluded for faith, of placing himself above God in attempting to conceive of this greater" (p. 77). Likewise, "God is he who, revealing himself as Creator, is called *quo maius cogitari nequit* and therefore who immediately confronts us

with his Name as the one who forbids us to conceive a greater
than him" (p. 169). The element of command in Barth's interpretation of the name of God, the engagement of the divine
will and the will of the believer, is brought out in Barth's remark that man recognizes "the embargo contained in the name
of God" and that he recognizes it "precisely in the limitation of
his freedom of thought." Even piety and morality, says Barth,
must be "directed towards establishing an absolute limitation
on this, the most inward and most intimate area of freedom"
(p. 169).

There are both similarities and differences between Barth's
reading of Anselm's *Proslogion* and the interpretation we have
given. The Christian distinction between God and the world
does leave the believer with a sense of God that does not possess the worldly contrasts, distinctions, and forms of otherness
that lie at the base of definitions of things in the world. God is
not differentiated, specifically, from human beings or animals
or inanimate things, and there are no generic similarities and
specific differences that allow us to comprehend him as we
comprehend the various kinds of beings. But the distinction of
God as creator from the world as created means that we have
something like an understanding of God. The special contrast at
work in this case gives us something like knowledge. The name
of God is not just a command never to think of anything
greater than him; the phrase "that than which nothing greater
can be thought" gives us an inkling of what God is, by implying
that even if the world or any being were added to him, the
result is nothing better or greater than God alone. This tells us
about God; it does not merely tell us what we are to avoid
thinking and how we are to restrain our freedom of thought.
We restrain our "freedom" of thought, not because of an injunction, but because of an understanding, or at least the
glimpse of an understanding.

Theology is situated beyond the difference between theoretical and practical science, but it does enjoy a theoretical aspect;
indeed St. Thomas says it is "more speculative than practical"
(*Summa theologiae* I q. 1, art. 4). Even the original understanding
of God as distinguished from the world has a speculative as

well as a practical dimension; it is not, as Barth seems to claim,
primarily a matter of obedience to a command. And yet we can
see how Barth could easily mistake the name of God for a
command. Anselm's formulation makes it clear that God is not
a kind of thing in the world, not even one of the divine things
in the world, and it appears therefore that there is nothing left
for the understanding to appropriate. In addition, faith and
obedience to God are in practice obviously necessary to question the world seriously in the way Christian belief questions it
and contrasts it to God's goodness and greatness. But if the
world or the whole is appreciated as the "other" to the creator,
and if the special adjustments of negation, causality, relation,
and being that must be made are made, then the understanding
that functions in this domain, with all the limitations and
obscurity it possesses, can be admitted. Each element —
negation, causality, relation; sameness and otherness; presence
and absence; rest and motion — simply has to be formulated in
terms appropriate to this singular context. Such analysis, as
negative and restricted as it might be, is theological thinking. It
is about the world and also about God, not just about our
thinking and our imagining.

   We have contrasted our interpretation of Anselm's text with
Thomistic approaches to the existence of God, with the transcendental method, and with Barth's reading of Anselm. The
Thomistic approach elaborates the metaphysics of *esse*, but it
does not focus sufficiently on the contrast between such
metaphysics and the pagan philosophy of being. The transcendental method is an attempt to shift the issue of being or
of *esse* to the issue of the questioning of being or *esse*; it turns its
attention to the investigator and to the inquiry into being. It
acknowledges the Kantian reserve concerning a straightforward
metaphysics and attempts to work with what escapes the Kantian critique: it turns from things to the subjectivity that desires
and knows things. Barth's approach is to have done with
metaphysics and to see the name of God as a command that
brings religious clarity but leaves us in philosophical darkness.
Our interpretation of Anselm makes an issue of the contrast
between the setting of Christian belief and the setting for sim-

ply natural reason. It remains with the issue of being, the world, *esse*, and God, and interprets the self only within this larger whole. And while acknowledging the restrictions on what can be known about God, it maintains that the distinction between God and the world provides an element of understanding. The issue of creation, at the intersection of faith and reason, permits us to think about God at least with the slight appreciations that analogy provides. The response to the name of God is not simply a submission of the will; there is something of an acknowledgment of what he is, and without this understanding there would be no reason to live as a Christian.

But these contrasts with other positions still do not answer the question whether Anselm's proof works as a proof. From the idea of God as that than which nothing greater can be thought can we infer that "such a nature" must indeed exist? From what we have said, it seems clear that this proof ought not to be taken as an illation from an idea to the existence of a being. When taken in this way, the argument seems somehow deceptive and unsatisfying. The real issue in Anselm's argument is whether or not being can be so understood that the world or the whole can be distinguished from God, and distinguished in such a way that the world or the whole might not have been, with no diminution of God's goodness or greatness. Is this distinction meaningful, is it thinkable, is it possible? If it is meaningful, thinkable, and possible, then the substantial theological-philosophical move has been made. To go on to infer the actual existence of God is merely to clarify an implication; the nerve of the argument is not in showing the actuality of God but in disclosing his possibility. In this domain real possibility involves actuality.[8] And the appreciation of the possibility of God is not simply the dawning of an idea in our minds; it is the appreciation of the world and everything in it in a new way. It begins with an involvement with beings, not in a reflective withdrawal from things.

But how is the possibility of this understanding of God and the world to be established? Is an argument needed at this point of Anselm's proof? Is the simple fact that some people say they look at the world this way enough to show that the world can truly be appreciated in this fashion? Clearly what is needed is the disclosure of a possibility in being, not simply a human claim. And the disclosure is not something that is communicated by a casual statement of terms. It is more like the disclosures needed to respond to questions like Is my life my own? Have I truly led my life or was it led for me? Is there a sense in which I can say, "I was meant to be"? Such questions do not permit a flip yes or no answer, and the very formulation of the question is itself the first and major possession of intelligibility in such matters. These questions and answers are not so cleanly differentiated as they are in questions about facts or the verification of hypothetical laws. This is not to say that we have no comprehension in such issues, but it is to say that the elusiveness of both the issue and any response to it must be appreciated. The question whether the world and God can be understood as Anselm and other Christian believers understand them is of this sort.

But on the other hand, because the distinction made here occurs between the world and God as not a part of the world, there is no experience, perception, or emotion that will serve to settle, objectively, the question whether the world can be conceived as created. There is no feeling of finitude or experience of dependence that gives an answer to such a question. It is true that personal experiences and sentiments, a sense of gratitude or regret or consolation or strength, may be very important in one's own religious and Christian history; but the Christian distinction itself cannot be based on such experiences and sentiments. It is not disclosed by them, and it can be achieved in the midst of different experiences, or with no sentiments at all. It is something thinkable, and hence it can be conveyed to others who have had a different emotional or personal constitution. Furthermore, because God is contrasted with the world, any scientific methodology that explores regions in the world will not directly either confirm or negate the Christian understanding of God. To appeal to psychology or cosmogony, to anthropology or biology, to animal evolution or to theories of an expanding universe, would be to miss the point of the issue. The Christian sense of God raises a question about the whole that is asked by no science, because each science works with possibilities within the whole.

Moreover, the Christian distinction between God and the world is not originally brought forward in speculation about conceivabilities; indeed there is something impious about treating it simply as an intellectual puzzle. In this it resembles distinctions like those between freedom and necessity and virtue and vice. The Christian distinction is first brought forward in life and activity, and ultimately it was first brought forward, it was first rendered, in the life of Christ. It continues to be made visible primarily in the Christian life. Flannery O'Connor, in one of her letters, describes someone who wrote to a friend "and asked him how he could possibly learn to believe, expecting, I suppose, a metaphysical answer. [His friend] only said, 'Give alms'."[9] And the understanding of the world as created, once proposed, is not a matter about which one can be unconcerned. It raises a question which calls not only for an intellectual assent or denial but also for a moral response. If God is understood as creator, one cannot be indifferent to him. Even a denial of his being takes on the tone of a rejection. This possibility of responding to God, understood as creator and redeemer, is kept alive by the church and by the lives of Christians. And yet this possibility becomes available for others precisely because there is an element of understanding in it: what is offered to others is not just association in a community or the chance to imitate someone's behavior or the opportunity to share in certain perceptions. It is the possibility of thinking about God and the world in a certain way and of living the faith that provides, nourishes, and completes this understanding. The Christian understanding involves a distinction, and hence it involves an element of thinking. If it did not present this element of thinking, it would make a demand that could not really be communicated to others.

There are times when the attempt to maintain the Christian sense of God provokes conflicts and even persecution. Persecution is not only motivated by reasons of political expedience or public order; there are cases when it becomes a violent form of rejecting the sense of God and of the world that is presented in

the Christian life. In such circumstances belief in God defines
itself not only in contrast to the philosophical exploration of
the world as the final context for thinking and acting but also in
contrast to unbelief in its most hostile form. The aura of this
possibility of violent rejection has always accompanied the determination of what God is and what demands the Christian
distinction makes on those who acknowledge it; it is present in
the Gospels themselves and in the early history of the church.
The possibility of martyrdom is not an incidental feature of
Christian understanding; it determines the extent of Christian
belief. In ancient Christian spirituality martyrdom was considered the highest possible expression of charity, the most faith-
ful imitation of Christ, and the closest form of union with him.
It became the pattern for other forms of Christian dedication
such as penitence, chastity, monastic solitude, or heroic
generosity, which were considered as a kind of equivalent to
martyrdom and were measured against it.[10] These are ways of
imitating Christ, and they express in action the truth that God
is distinct from the world, that the goods and necessities of the
world and of human life are not final when they are seen in
contrast to the God who created and redeemed us.

As powerful as such witnesses to Christian faith may be,
they still require as part of their sense the Christian distinction
between God and the world and the understanding that this
distinction provides. We do not simply admire the courage,
charity, and dedication of heroic Christian lives; in and through
these lives, and in and through the Gospels and the teaching of
the church, we are invited to understand God in a certain way.
This distinction between God and the world cannot be established by any prior premises. Any argument to display the distinction is rather a clarification of what the distinction means.
There is a constant need to render the distinction again and
again, to clarify and contrast it against ever new things with
which it might be confused. The activity of sustaining our grasp
of this distinction is part of the teaching function of the church,
but it is also the center of what is to be done in theological
thinking. Different historical circumstances will bring pressure
to bear on the distinction from different directions: at one time

it will be Christological controversy, at another the sacraments or the liturgy, at another grace and human action, at another issues of psychology or language or the sciences of nature. Theological thinking in response to such issues is essentially contrastive. But although the tide of history will bear on Christian understanding from various directions, the distinction itself is not simply the expression of one historical point of view. What occurs in Anselm's argument is not to be explained away by Anselm's penchant for "turning within" as opposed to a liking for "empirical" studies. It is not to be reduced to its historical conditions, and it is so reduced only by writers who cannot do more than narrate historical circumstances. Precisely because the Christian distinction expressed in Anselm's writing questions the world or the whole, it is not reducible to one more of the shifting perspectives within the whole. There is in Anselm, and in the Christian appreciation of the world, something to be always understood and repeated, a distinction to be made again now and preserved for repetition in the future.[11]

NOTES

1. Reply to Gaunilo, part 2.

2. Gaunilo's response *Pro insipiente*, paragraphs 2 and 4.

3. See Robert Sokolowski, "Making Distinctions," *The Review of Metaphysics* 32 (1979): 652 – 61.

4. Bernard Lonergan, *Insight: A Study of Human Understanding* (New York: Longmans, Green and Co., 1957), p. 672.

5. Ibid., pp. 673 – 77.

6. Karl Rahner, for example, frequently speaks of the luminosity of being, the human anticipation (*Vorgriff*) of the infinite, and the human potential to hear the word of God. See the passages from *Hearers of the Word* in the new translation by Joseph Donceel in *A Rahner Reader*, edited by Gerald A. McCool (New York: Seabury, 1975), pp. 2 – 64.

7. Karl Barth, *Anselm: Fides Quaerens Intellectum*, translated by I.W. Robertson (London: SCM Press, 1960).

8. In the *Opus Oxoniense* and the *De primo principio* Scotus bases his argument for the existence of God on the possibility that God exists. He claims that he has simply touched up Anselm's argument. For a clear introductory description of Scotus' proof see Armand A. Maurer, *Medieval Philosophy* (New York: Random House, 1964), pp. 222 – 27.

9. Flannery O'Connor, *The Habit of Being*, letters edited and with an introduction by Sally Fitzgerald (New York: Farrar, Straus, Giroux, 1979), p. 164.

10. See Gustave Thils, *Sainteté Chrétienne* (Tielt: Editions Lannoo, 1958), p. 308.

11. For a further comparison between Thomistic metaphysical doctrines and the Christian distinction as we have described it see Appendix II.

10. Reading the Scriptures

How are we to read the Bible? Whether we read it privately, or with others, or for others, how are we to make our own what is written in the scriptures? A theological question arises today in the reading of scripture because of what we might call an embarrassment of riches; there is so much historical and philological information, so many parallels in other literary traditions, and so many distinctions to be made in the body of the text itself, between original and modified formulations, between authentic words and attributed speeches, between passages coming from different hands and reflecting different theologies, that the sense of the Bible as one book becomes questioned in a way it was never questioned before. Furthermore, it is often said that we no longer live in the "world" the Bible talks about, that the world defined by the Bible, and taken for granted by it, is not congruent with ours.

The center of the Christian scriptures is the narration of the life of Christ. The New Testament tells us what Jesus did and what he said. However, this narration also involves, necessarily, a report of what those who encountered Christ did and said; Christ acts and speaks with others and responds to them, and they to him. Both the agent and the respondent must be described when an action is narrated. But in addition, the New Testament also presents the actions and words of people who live, so to speak, in the wake of Christ: it shows how people live who believe in Christ but have not seen him. It also describes how others who may not believe in Christ react toward those who do. This expression of the Christian life in the absence of Christ is found in the Acts of the Apostles, in the Epistles, and in the Apocalypse. It also affects the formulations and emphases of the Gospel narratives themselves, most explicitly in passages in which Christ speaks in anticipation of those who have not seen but still believe. The New Testament thus presents two concentric groups surrounding Christ, one made up of those who react to his direct presence and another made up of those who are defined in their relation to him in his absence.

To someone trained as a historian it might appear that the most urgent scholarly task in New Testament studies would be to determine the very words and actions of Christ and to distinguish them from additions and interpretations that others made later. This might permit us to reconstruct an original core for the Gospels and to measure the later modifications, as well as the later forms of Christian life, against what preceded them. It would permit a criticism within the New Testament itself. Such a task is, of course, extremely difficult to carry out, but we may also ask whether it is desirable in principle. Christ did not speak and act by himself; he spoke and acted with and toward others. And no one speaks until he has been understood; the understanding of Christ's words achieved by those who heard him and by those who thought about him after he left is the completion of the speaking of Christ. The disciples complete the words of Jesus by responding to them. Likewise, no one acts except in the impact of his action, and the impact of what Christ did was not rounded out until it was appreciated in the lives of those who did not see the action but who believed in it. The New Testament presents not only the life of Jesus but also the reaction and response of those who experienced his life, and the reaction and response of those who believed in him without encountering him; what he said and did had to be responded to in these two ways, and once the two reactions were accomplished, a kind of closure was reached. The essential ways of reacting to Christ were portrayed, and the words and deeds of Christ were shown in the effect they can have. This is not to say that the New Testament depicts all the various ways in which different kinds of people, with differ-

ent temperaments and cultures, might respond to Christ; but it
is to say that the more formal possibilities, of reacting to him
in his immediate presence and of reacting to him in his absence, have been sketched. From then on it becomes a matter
of repetition, not the opening of a new dimension. In respect to
showing the formal possibilities of reacting and responding tò
Christ, and for the purpose of understanding the presence and
absence of Christ, we and our contemporaries are less different
from the Corinthians or the Thessalonians than the Corinthians
and the Thessalonians were from those who knew Christ
directly.

The scriptures are read in the absence of Christ. Whenever
they are to be read again in different historical circumstances,
the problem of interpretation arises. One of the tasks of Christian theology is to show that what the Bible says can be asserted as true in the world in which the reader lives. This
apologetic function of theology has a rhetorical dimension: it is
necessary to take into account the mind of the audience being
addressed and to discover the forms of argument best suited to
it. In fact the assumption generally made in the world in which
we live is that the experts in truth, the judges of what is real
and ultimately credible, are the scientists. There is a tendency,
therefore, for those who study the Bible to want to show its
truth by letting their study of it comply with scientific criteria.
No one attempts any longer to make the Bible appear true
according to the standards and methods of the natural sciences,
like physics, biology, medicine, or astronomy, because, it is
said, the Bible and the natural sciences are involved in different
undertakings. But although it may not be a treatise "on the
universe," the Bible is definitely a historical writing. Thus it is
tempting for biblical scholars to try to show that the Bible can
be reconciled with modern science by showing that the study of
the Bible can conform to the most exacting criteria of historical
method. But, of course, such a historical treatment of the Bible
will not make it capable of being affirmed and appropriated. In
addition to using philological and historical criticism, biblical
theologians must "apply" the Bible to the world in which they
live: not simply by showing how the moral lessons of the Bible

can be carried out in their circumstances but also by showing how what the Bible asserts is repeatable as true.

An important part of such demonstration is, clearly, to live according to what the scriptures say. The scriptures are a message of salvation, and the primary way they are applied is by accepting the salvation presented in them. But an element of thinking and distinguishing is required for this, since misunderstandings about what the scriptures mean can raise impediments to living the scriptural message. The most fundamental intellectual requirement for understanding the Bible is that it be read in the light of the Christian distinction between God and the world. If this is not done, the salvation promised in the scriptures is almost bound to be distorted. Without this distinction we may, for example, try to interpret the Bible as simply revealing dimensions of human existence, such as ultimate concern, futurity, the conflict between reason and passion, or the emergence of reason in history.[1] Also, without this distinction the metaphorical and symbolic elements in the Bible spin out of control. There is no basis on which to determine what is literal and what is metaphorical or symbolic.

But do the scriptures themselves provide us with this distinction, in the light of which they are to be read? The scriptures tell us especially about salvation: about God's love for the world and for men, about his justice, about the kingdom of God, and about the redemption brought about by Christ. As a setting for this love and salvation, the Bible also says that God created the world and that everything comes from him, that he is indebted to no one and to nothing. But the Bible does not formulate the relationship between God and the world in the metaphysical terms we find in Anselm and Aquinas. The Bible may say "Heaven and earth are mine, says the Lord," but it does not say explicitly that God could have been all that he is even if he had not created the world. The Bible tells us what God has done, not what would have been the case if he had not done it. But this further claim, that God could be all that he is had the world not existed, is needed to determine what occurs in creation, providence, and redemption. The sense in which heaven and earth are "God's own," the sense in which we are to live as sons of God, needs this distinction in order to be appropriately determined.

Do we then have to go beyond the scriptures to obtain the light under which the scriptures are to be read? Do we have to obtain the most fundamental distinction needed for reading the Bible from a source other than the Bible itself? It is not the case that the only thing in the Bible are statements telling us about God; the Bible also contains a narration of events, and these events can contain the Christian distinction without explicitly formulating it. In the events narrated and appreciated in the New Testament the Christian distinction is lived by Christ. The distinction that displays God and the world for what they ultimately are is lived by Jesus in a more accurate and effective way than it is anywhere formulated. The Christian distinction between God and the world is the kind of thing that has to be lived before it can be stated. In the life of Jesus the world is questioned in a way it is not questioned by philosophy. The world is questioned and brought to light in contrast to the God who can remain God while becoming man, and whose divinity and action are made manifest not only in a teaching but in the crucifixion and resurrection. The sense of God that comes forward for us in these events is that of the God who could become part of the world, as man, without disrupting the integrity of the world and of nature; he must therefore not be one of the kinds of being in the world. And when we reflect on what this implies, we see that he could not be a God who requires anything in the world to be himself or to be in any way better or greater. There are many statements in the scriptures that assert the independence and the dominion of God, but the full force of such statements is appreciated only when they are taken together with the events that were accomplished in the life of Christ.

The Christian distinction between God and the world is most vividly asserted in the actions and events that present it, not primarily in the words that make it known. The words alone without the events have a kind of "bookish" flavor: as in the case of freedom and necessity or virtue and vice, we have not accomplished the distinction most completely when we formulate it in words. It remains incomplete, empty, and almost eccentric if it is only stated and not lived by the one who formulates it. For this reason it is quite true that the imitation of Christ in the life of the Christian is the primary and proper repetition of the Christian distinction between God and the world. The need to imitate Christ — by acceptance of God's will, by acts of charity toward others, by renunciation of worldly goods for the sake of the kingdom of God, by forgiveness, and by prayer and the sacramental life — is not simply a matter of pious exhortation or moral excellence; it is based on the kinds of events that occurred in the life of Jesus, on the distinctions that were brought out in those events. It is based on the "nature" of the things made manifest in Christ. We cannot hear about these realities without, simultaneously, being called to imitate them and to involve ourselves with them. They are not things that can only be contemplated. It may not be one of the functions of theology to exhort others to believe in Christ and to imitate him; it may not be one of the functions of theology to preach. Preaching as such may be considered a supplement to theological reflection. But theology may have an even more intimate connection with the imitation of Christ than preaching does, in that it must show the necessity of action and imitation in response to the life of Christ. It must show the ground for preaching; it must show why preaching is not an accessory but part of the very presence and reality of the Christian distinction.

We have been emphasizing the Christian distinction between God and the world; how is this distinction related to what is achieved in the Old Testament? To what extent does the Old Testament already present God as creator? Certainly the Old Testament establishes that there is only one God, in contrast to the many gods of the gentiles, and clearly it forbids any image of God, in contrast to the idolatries of other peoples. Not only in the creation narratives but also in the psalms and in the prophets God is said to have made everything, and the heavens and earth are said to be his. The frequent teaching about divine providence, as it occurs in the election of Israel, in the guidance of Israel through the events that occur in its history, and in the

knowledge that God has of each one even before he was conceived and no matter where he goes, implies a very pure notion
of how God creates and sustains the world. It may even be
claimed that the Old Testament developed the teaching that
God created the world out of nothing. The claim that God
selects certain people, that he chooses to reveal himself in a
certain place and to some particular individual, that he inter-
venes in particular events, implies a kind of dominion over the
world which is different from the general governance and
unification which are the work of the pagan god. The world is
somehow at the disposition of God. If God can do the things he
is said to do in the Old Testament, he is divine in a way different from the way the god of Aristotle, Plato, or the Stoics is
divine, and his relationship to the world is different. Even in the
Old Testament, therefore, the saving action of God sheds light
on how his creation of the world is to be understood.

Moreover, the God of the Old Testament is not unrelated to
what the pagans worship. When the Jewish writers speak of
God, they speak of "the same thing" that the gentiles speak of
with their god and gods, except that the Jews consider themselves to be speaking truly while the others are in error. The
others worship false gods, or they worship God falsely. The
God of the Old Testament is the truth of what the pagans
anticipate when they think they respond to the divine.

And it is the God of the Old Testament who is the figure
behind the events and teachings of the New Testament. He is
the Father by whom Jesus says he has been sent, the Father
whose will he does. Jesus understands himself within the tradition of the Hebrew scriptures and the understanding of God
developed in them. He presents himself to his hearers, and to
those who react and respond to him, within the sense of God
that has emerged in "what has been written." This understanding and presentation are not just psychological or mental things;
they are the disclosure of how Jesus exists in his mission and in
his origin and in what he does. Furthermore, the church, too,
appreciates Christ within the setting of the Old Testament. The
use the apostles make of the prophets is not just an apologetical or rhetorical device to persuade people to believe in Christ;

it is also an understanding of what occurred in Jesus, a presentation of the full sense of his actions.

In accepting Christ against the setting of the God of the
scriptures, the God whom Christ called Father, the church also
appreciates the relationship between what the pagans look for
when they seek the divine and what Christ has brought when
he proclaimed the kingdom of God. As we read in the Acts of
the Apostles and in the letters of Paul, especially Romans and
Galatians, the earliest controversies in the church, the earliest
need for distinctions, concerned how the pagans were to accept
the kingdom of God: Could they accept the Gospel only by first
living the sense of God and redemption presented in the Old
Testament? Would any other access be closed to them? Or was
it possible to enter the faith directly, so to speak, as a
fulfillment of what the pagans look for when they look for god?
This early argument was not just a matter of ceremonials, and
its resolution was a distinction which brought about a new interpretation of the Old Testament. It was decided that the
ceremonial law was not binding on converts from paganism,
but these converts were still to be considered as children of
Abraham, whose true paternity was now to be taken to be
founded on faith and not on the law, and who is to be the
father of many nations and not just one (Romans 4). Thus,
while the ceremonials and the law are considered to be un-
necessary (because they were completed, not because they were
wrong), the prophetic tradition must be sustained. Although the
life of Jesus completes the Old Testament, and the faith of the
New Testament completes the faith of the Old, the life and
teaching of Jesus can be appreciated only as completing what
was done in the tradition within which he lived. The resolution
of the early controversy regarding the law did not simply reject
the law; it also interpreted the law and the Old Testament in
such a way that they still remain remembered as the expectation to which Christ is the completion. And for Christians this
means that the life of Christ is not a kind of unique event that
has no setting and can be determined in no way; the presence
of Christ is to be understood within the sense of God provided
by the Old Testament and even within the sense of the divine

possessed by pagans. The divinity of Christ surpasses the anticipations which it completes, but it presents itself only within the setting they provide.

The Old Testament teaches the oneness, the independence, and the creative dominion of God. But when the distinction between faith and the law is made, does it affect the sense we have of the God who is served either in faith or under the law? When Jesus is understood as being the Son of God, when the Word is understood as both being with God and being God, is the sense of what God is and what creation is thereby modified? If God is now appreciated not only as capable of determining particular events and manifestations in the world but also as being able to become part of the the world, in Christ, is the sense of the relationship between God and the world changed? Are both God and the world understood differently in their relationship to one another? The Christian understanding does not negate the understanding of God achieved in the Old Testament, but it is also not the simple acceptance, without modification and adjustment, of the Old Testament sense of God as Father and as creator.

As an example, if God is to be able to become man without distorting human nature, then human nature, and nature as such, must be appreciated as maintaining its integrity before God. In the Old Testament natural phenomena were taken to be what they are because God chose them to be thus and so. This teaching helps us appreciate God's creative power, his independence of the world, and his dominion over it. It makes the Hebrew God different from the gods who are part of the world. But this very "interventionist" conception of God in his relation to nature is surpassed by the conception of God in the New Testament as allowing things to be according to their own natures, and yet remaining their creator and lord in the sense of letting them exist. The insistence on the natural makes the otherness of God more profound; God is more radically contrasted to nature than he is in the Old Testament. The doctrine of the incarnation, with its emphasis on the integrity of the human being of Christ, brings out this deeper sense of God as creator. Likewise, the prohibition of images of God in the Old

Testament was needed to emphasize that God cannot even be represented as part of the world. It stressed his difference from the world and his independence of it. But the acceptance of images in Christianity implies a more radical difference between God and things, because it assumes that even if an image or an icon is made, God's otherness is such that it is not contaminated.

Furthermore, in the Old Testament the law plays a central role in man's response to God. It is true that the prophets emphasized internal attitudes, virtues, justice, and a service that went beyond the law, but the law remained as an element in the service of God. In the New Testament the law is surpassed in a way in which it was not surpassed by the prophets. Because of who Christ was and because of what he accomplished (which he did not accomplish by virtue of the law) there would by sacraments and not ceremonials, faith and not the law. The God who is to be worshipped apart from the law is not understood in exactly the same way as the God of the law. It is not simply that different attributes of God are to be stressed, like his mercy instead of his justice; such shifts of emphasis occurred even in the Old Testament. Rather, the divinity of God is differently understood. The Christian emphasis on the integrity of nature, it may be added, does not stem simply from the historical circumstance that Greek notions of nature were introduced into Christianity and served to supplement the oriental notion of God's absolute power over the world: it derives rather from the incarnation as the central occurrence in Christian history, and from the implications the incarnation has for our understanding of both God and nature.

The deepening of the understanding of God that occurs in the New Testament is involved in the general understanding Christians have of the New Testament as completing the anticipations of the Old. The New Testament does not merely fulfill prophecies about the Messiah; there are many symbols, events, and statements in the Old Testament that become taken as anticipations of something beyond themselves, like the manna in the desert, the bronze serpent, the Passover, and the deliverance of the Jews from captivity in Egypt. Such words, it has

been said, have a "fuller sense," a *sensus plenior*, and such events
and things serve as "types" of something beyond themselves.
They are a saying or a doing whose sense is not fully exhausted
by its own circumstances but is determined by what occurs in
the New Testament.

When we think about prophecies, types, and the *sensus
plenior*, we ought not let the particularities of each case — like
Isaiah's prophecy of the virgin giving birth, or the prophecies of
the suffering servant, or the bronze serpent raised by
Moses — to allow us to overlook the fact that the more basic
fulfillment achieved in the New Testament is the deeper sense
of God, as the God who can become man: this is the decisive
fulfillment, and it provides the setting within which the other
more particular fulfillments occur. Because of it the other
prophecies and signs are anticipations and not just forecasts. It
is not simply the event that a virgin will bear a child, or that
someone will come who will bear our guilt, or even that someone will be raised up and put to death for our sins, that is in
itself the decisive issue and fulfillment. What is most fundamental and most completing is that the sense of everything, of
God and the world, of innocence and guilt, is so adjusted that
the incarnation and the redemption can take place. This adjustment, as well as the incarnation and the redemption, can be
seen to be anticipated by the Old Testament, but the sense of
the anticipation itself is only appreciated in retrospect, when it
is fulfilled. The actions of God in the New Testament are the
actions of the God who could be all that he is, in undiminished
goodness and greatness, even if there were no world. And of
course the fulfillment does not make the prophecies and symbols otiose, because there must be an anticipation of sense if
there is to be any manifestation of sense at all. Even when we
appreciate the fulfillment now, we understand it as completing
an anticipation.

This understanding of God makes it possible for Christians
to pray with the words of the psalms and the words of the
prophets. The prayer that wind and rain, snow and hail, day
and night, should praise God, or that God will protect the just
and bring down the wicked, that he upholds the mountains,

stills the roaring sea, and sends rain on the earth, or that all our ways lie open to him, that he knows what we will say before the word is on our tongue, and that neither in distance nor in darkness can we be where he is not — all these things, if read against the Christian understanding of God as creator and the corresponding Christian sense of the world and of ourselves, are not just attractive metaphors or poetic embellishment; they have something literal in them, something that we can assert and pray in truth. However, if such things are not read against this understanding of God, they lose that core of literalness and repeatability and become antiquated and bound to the cultural milieu in which they arose.

The theology of disclosure can help us discuss more adequately the differences that occur in biblical revelation. Thus, if the incarnation reveals a more intense meaning of God's otherness to the world than the writings of the Old Testament revealed, the attention we pay to the form of disclosure will prevent us from simply projecting back into the Old Testament the sense of creation achieved in the New. The stages of manifestation are acknowledged and their differences are registered as truly and somehow necessarily there; they are not taken as mere historical accidents. Even the "fullest sense" is seen as needing to be contrasted and differentiated, in its manifestation if not in its being in itself, from the less complete senses. Moreover, the differences and relationships in the realm of disclosure are elusive. We deal, not with the emergence of new attributes of what is disclosed, but with a new sense or dimension of attributes that are already there. God is the creator and lord of the world in the Old Testament, but the sense of creation and dominion is adjusted when God is seen as being able to become man, or when the world is seen as being able to accept the incarnation. What is added is a set of new contrasts in which the same appears in a new light; it is not that the same appears as something different from what it was. The theology of the things revealed, taken by itself, does not elaborate sufficient distinctions and does not work from the appropriate perspective to do justice to the analyses that are here called for.

In addition, the kind of reflective thinking that makes manifestation, or presences and absences, its theme is able to develop appropriate categories and distinctions for a philosophical treatment of things like language, speech, thinking, wisdom, and appearance. When such terms are used in the scriptures, when Christ is called the Logos, or when we are told that God spoke and all things were made, or when other topics of disclosure, like "face" or "being with" or "memory," or "epiphany" or "name," or even "faith" and "hope," are used in the narration of God's involvement with the world, a theology of disclosure may be able to bring out more of the sense of such passages and, again, bring out more of their literal meaning. It can make them capable of being appropriated in a more literal sense. We would not be left with a merely historical explanation, like being told that the ancient Hebrews thought that anyone who knew the name of something had a kind of power over it. We could be shown what it is in naming that made the ancients think that way, and we may be able to see that some of these dimensions of disclosure still hold now. The theological reflection on presencing makes it possible to take more things in the Bible seriously and not just as positions once held by others; we do not have to understand them only in terms of their historical circumstances. The theology of manifestation can bring out both biblical and patristic truths that have been neglected because of the philosophical attitude toward appearances that has prevailed in recent centuries.

There is one more question that should be raised concerning the theology of disclosure and the interpretation of scripture. We have stressed that the Bible tells us what God has done, not what he might have done. Theological speculation should also reflect on what God has actually willed, not on what he could will: it should think about his *volitum*, not his *velle*. The reason for this is that we simply do not know what else God might have done; there would be no control over our imagination. For example, God willed to become man in order to redeem man from sin. There was sin, and Christ was sent to redeem us from it. Whether the redemption could have been done in another way, or whether the incarnation could have occurred under other circumstances or for other purposes, is not a proper topic for theology. Even the claim that the incarnation could have been willed simply for the glory of God is not for us to make, since in fact the glory of God in the incarnation occurs in the redemption from sin.

Yet a question may arise concerning our formulation of the relationship between God and the world. Are we not speculating about the simple *velle* of God rather than about his *volitum*? Have we not said what God would be like if he had not created the world, and have we not thereby violated this principle of theological moderation? Have we not admitted that the statement "God is all that there is" is contrary to fact and yet meaningful, and have we not thereby spoken about what could be but in fact is not? The response to this objection is that the possibility that God could be all that there is is not another action, another possible *volitum* that God could have performed; we are not projecting imaginatively something else, some positive alternative, that God might have accomplished. We project the possibility of the world's not existing, not to suggest another world, but to determine the sense of the world that does exist. We assert that the world need not have been, which is the same as saying that it exists as a result of choice; we do not say what else there might have been instead of the world. The negation we propose is too rudimentary and too simple in what it achieves to violate the rule that theologically we can think about what God willed and not about what he could have willed: our remarks establish the sense of the world as willed; they do not speculate about what else God might have chosen to do.

NOTE

1. For example, see Kant's "Conjectural Beginning of Human History," translated by Emil L. Fackenheim and included in *On History*, edited by Lewis White Beck (Indianapolis: Bobbs-Merrill, 1963); and Hegel, *Lectures on the Philosophy of Religion*, translated by E.B. Spiers and J. Burdon Sanderson (New York: Humanities, 1962), vol. 2, pp. 341 – 46; vol. 3, pp. 81 – 100, 112 – 23.

11. Christian Experience

Are there Christian experiences? Is the object of Christian faith ever presented to us directly, in one of the many forms of perceiving that occur in the experience of the world? Could Christian faith be founded on someone's perception? In our natural experience there are a variety of kinds of perception, and different kinds of things are presented in each. We can distinguish among visual, auditory, and tactile experiences; we can distinguish among political, aesthetic, moral, and religious experiences; we can distinguish among the experiences of music, of drama, and of paintings. Each experience is correlated to its kind of object; there are differences not only in the ways of experiencing but in the objects made available in them. And there can be overlaps; a political experience may involve visual and auditory elements, and a religious experience may also involve an aesthetic perception. In such cases the thing presented has different aspects in what it presents to us.

Is there one kind among the many kinds of experiencing that is specifically Christian? Is there a special perception of the Christian God? Do we enjoy an experience in which the Christian God is "given" or made present? In the strict sense is there a theophany of the Christian God? There are, of course, some experiences that seem obviously to be Christian, like taking part in the sacraments; addressing in prayer God the Father, the Son, and the Holy Spirit; bringing the events of the New Testament to mind; expressing faith, hope, and charity; acting in the imitation of Christ; or being engaged in an action of the church. But if the Christian God is not a part of the world, there is a sense in which we cannot hope to perceive or experience him, because he would have to be presented as one of the kinds of things in the world, differentiated from other kinds, and the experience that presents him would have to be differentiated from our other perceptions. Some writers have appealed to extraordinary experiences, like moments of great suffering or great happiness, of ecstasy or of a basic reappraisal of our lives, as special perceptions that make us aware of the divine. Are such experiences, which may call into question the very "world" in which we have lived, to be considered presentations of the Christian God, and can faith be founded on them?

As a setting for the discussion of this problem, we must examine natural human experience. Although there are different kinds of perceptions giving us different kinds of objects, there are no absolutely raw, uninterpreted, unarticulated givens in experience. Any givenness involves some interpretative performance on the part of the "dative" to whom the object is given. We always must do things in making the object present. Even on the simple level of perceiving objects by vision or by touch we must move around in certain ways to perceive anything as an independent object. Even feelings require a sense of anticipation and recognition, a continuous process of identifying, and an articulation in which both things outside us and we ourselves are distinguished from our sensibility. More complex perceptions require more complex interpretation. To recognize a tree as a tree involves memory, language, and perceptual identification; to make a tool present to us as a tool requires becoming able to use tools. Still more complex linguistic and thoughtful interpretation is needed to perceive such things as political, moral, aesthetic, or administrative objects, like seeing the inauguration of the president, watching someone outfox someone else, or being present when a judicial decision is made. We must involve a lot of language to "have" such objects "given" to us.

The involvement of language does not deprive what is given of its objectivity: there still remains the difference between actually seeing the inauguration and merely hearing about it;

between seeing the inauguration and seeing a picture of it; between seeing the true inauguration and seeing a deceptive facsimile; between seeing it with adequate appreciation of what is going on and seeing it confusedly. The presence of language does not turn everything into convention or subjectivity, and it does not turn everything into language. The fact that language permeates experience simply means that some objects — and most objects that are of importance to us — are complex and require articulation in order to be presented.

The interpretative dimension of our experience, both the linguistic and the nonlinguistic, comes almost entirely from the community in which we live. We assimilate from others our vocabulary and syntax, our skills and habits, and even the shape that our mobility assumes; we become ourselves first by drawing on others. Thus even the disclosures based on mobility and the use of tools come from our community; all the more do our linguistic abilities arise from it. And as we take in our language, we breathe in and out along with it the current and dominant opinions about things. Such linguistic assimilation underlies any original thinking and speaking we may be able to achieve. Written texts are only a part of this process of shaping our articulation of things; speech is more basic, and actions and behavior more basic still.

What then is to be said about Christian experience? To what extent is it articulated by language? To what extent is it the result of an interpretation of what we live through? Of course, no such thing as an unarticulated Christian "given" exists because there are no raw, unarticulated givens of any sort. All experience involves some anticipation and articulation, and if the experience is at all complex, it involves language.

Among the articulated human experiences one form can be called religious experience. There is not only a perception of places, events, and actions that can be called sacred; there is also a sense of something that is divine: a sense of the awesome, the overwhelming, that which calls for total dedication, that to which sacrifice is required, that which seems to be the origin of goodness and the discrimination of what is evil, that which is more powerful than anything human and has to do

with the origins of the human and the origins of the order we
experience, that from which we cannot run away, that which
comes and goes as it will. This is a special kind of experience,
and it presents a special kind of being, one differentiated from
the other kinds that are not divine. Even if the divine is thought
to pervade other things, it must be distinguished from them;
the divine appears as a part of what is, even though the highest
and most powerful part. Wherever the divine is to be placed,
whether in a plethora of gods, in a living force in nature, in a
self-thinking mind, or in something within the human spirit,
there is a religious experience and a religious perception that
makes it present; such experience must be differentiated from
the aesthetic, moral, political, and other sorts of human presentation.

The Christian sense of the divine is not simply equivalent to
what is made present in such religious perception. Christian
belief involves a natural sense of the divine, but it goes beyond
"the gods" and the human experience of them. God as creator
is not a part of the world, and he therefore cannot be experienced as part of it. Language is especially important in establishing this sense of the divine; we believe in God because we
have heard of him, from the church, from the Bible, and ultimately from Christ. Our faith and understanding of God are
not simply based on religious experience. Because of the unperceivability of God the teaching and the speech of the church
take on an importance greater than the interpretative importance of language and tradition in all human experience. We
could not expect human experience, for example, to "work
out" Christianity and the Christian distinction between God
and the world. There is a facticity, a necessary historical element in having the church somehow there to transmit the
words, message, and actions of Christ, together with the sense
of God that they imply.

This is why the church as a teacher is so important in
Christianity and why "dogmas" play so much a part in Christian tradition. The mystery of the church and the nature of its
teaching authority are related to the understanding of God and
the world reached in Christianity. There is no natural human

experience or perception, no achievement of philosophers or thoughtful persons, no artistic achievement, and no accomplishment of holy men, that could bring about the Christian life and the Christian distinction that is the articulation at the core of that life. The disclosures that occurred in the words and actions of Christ, and that were recorded as disclosures in the scriptures, were necessary to bring the Christian faith about. The need for revelation and for the church to preserve it stems not from sectarian claims of special enlightenment; it is based on what is proposed as the object of belief. Furthermore, Christianity is not just one more cultural form adopted by the religious instinct (although it is indeed also that). Christianity questions the world and understands God and his involvement in the world in such a way as to go beyond what the religious sense could present. It is not simply another articulation of the world or the whole, not simply one among many identifications of what we experience as divine.

Our reaction to Christian realities involves the natural religious instinct and the "object" that this instinct presents, but the Christian divinity surpasses such natural presences. As an example, in his commentary on Psalm 127 St. Hilary discusses natural human fear and says, "This fear then is not taught but comes from natural weakness. We do not learn what ought to be feared; rather, the things we fear themselves instill their own dread in us." But in contrast to this spontaneous fear, he says, "The fear of God is something to be learned, because it is taught. It is found not in fright, but in the way of teaching."[1] Analogously, the structures of natural religious experience do not, without "teaching," present Christian divinity; but they are allowed to remain intact, though purified, by the sense of the divine reached in Christianity. The object of Christian reverence does not exercise a special kind of impact on the passions and sensibility that would be comparable to, and differentiated from, the impression made by objects presented in wordly experience; there is no special Christian feeling. But Christian life does exercise the natural attitudes and sentiments in the light of Christian belief and in response to the God proclaimed in such faith.

It is necessary to maintain a judicious balance between the natural instinct and the Christian interpretation. Thus, one of the human concerns that is involved in religion is the concern with health and with the continuation of life. We pray for the healing of the sick, and Jesus accepted this aspect of religion during his life when he answered the prayers of many who were sick and crippled, blind and mute. And in the present, prayers for the sick, and prayers by the sick, are a part of the Christian life. But it is also possible to lose one's balance here and, either in the case of an individual or in the case of a sect, to turn Christianity into a kind of support for good health. Structures and behavior may develop in such a way that no context beyond that of good health — or perhaps security in life or financial success or military victory — is recognized. This constitutes a shift from Christian belief to the reverence of the necessities of life. We should be neither amused nor scandalized if such things happen. The natural necessities are always there with their insistence, and as human beings we are always quite inclined to bow, even religiously, before them. It requires careful attention to the integrity of doctrine to keep the Christian distinction intact and alive and in control of the natural religious instinct, not in the service of it.

Similarly, a person may express the conviction that "God wants me to be here, where I am now, to do what I can with and for those who are with me." This kind of sentiment need not, in itself, be Christian, and the experience or feeling it expresses is not a kind of perception of the divine will. It can be a religious recognition of that strange necessity that seems to bind us in our being to the place and time, family and society, context and history, in which we actually are. It can be a religious appreciation of a natural necessity. This sentiment of the necessity of our placement can of course be absorbed into the Christian belief in creation and into the understanding of God's providence implied by creation, but the Christian elements are not a further sensibility or feeling. They interpret the experience and purify it, but they are themselves acquired as beliefs by hearing the word of God and not by a perception. But they do shed light on the natural perceptions we have and bring out the full truth that is in them. Christian belief not only leaves intact abstract truths about the natural; it also enhances our experience of the necessity of things.

The blend between a natural perception and Christian interpretation can also occur in regard to more theoretical discourse or writing. There can be blends between intellectual fascination and Christian religious reverence, and it is always possible for us to mistake the intellectual experience for the Christian reaction. For example, in Christian writings we may be deeply impressed by the verbal structures or by the analysis of some natural pattern, like temporality, friendship, hope and futurity, or change and permanence, and we may suppose that our admiration is a kind of sense of the divine. But the impression made by such things when they are articulated can again be the religious reverence for things brought out and recognized as ultimate necessities in the world. We may be moved by Augustine's articulation of memory and think we are responding to something specifically Christian. Such reverent recognitions can, by themselves, simply be intellectual insight; if they are to be blended into the life of Christian belief, they must be made in the light of the Christian distinction between God and the world and with the faith, hope, and charity associated with that distinction.

Writers like Augustine succeed in exercising the disclosure of necessities within the context of faith; they bring out the natural, but they do so within Christian belief. If some other writers fail in this theological enterprise, their failure consists in allowing the disclosure of the natural necessity to stand simply on its own and to govern the way we interpret Christian faith and the Christian sense of God. They interpret the Christian in terms of the natural, instead of the natural in terms of the Christian. One example of this reversal would be the interpretation of eschatology as the expression of human futurity and progress; another would be the interpretation of creation as the living center of time, the origin of meaning and order in the world we experience. Still others might be the interpretation of God as the sum of the ideals that human beings project for themselves, and the interpretation of Christian faith as human authenticity.

In contrast to such reversals the successful theologian brings out natural necessities in the special light that Christian faith provides: a light that stems, not from one more intellectual intuition, similar in kind to philosophical or scientific insight, but from the Christian distinction between God and the world, with the particular blend of faith, action, and reason that this distinction requires.

The blend of intellect and faith has a parallel in the balance required between music and Christian prayer. A beautiful hymn may fill us with religious reverence; this is appropriate if the beauty of the song is in the service of our worship of God and if our reverence is directed toward the creator and redeemer. But it may be the melodic experience that really moves us, the aesthetic perception of a necessity of form, something analogous to our intellectual understanding of a natural necessity. Sometimes, indeed, the aesthetic attraction may be so great that the inappropriateness of the music or of the words of the song is not noticed, and the incongruity of singing it in a Christian church may not be perceived. *The Battle Hymn of the Republic*, that song to a modern version of Ares, is a good example of this; its bloodthirsty wrath, sword, and trumpet in the service of a particular army are quite out of place in a Christian setting, but its melody is so stirring and its phonemic patterns so attractive that the people who sing it most probably do not appreciate the meaning of the words they pronounce.

Because the Christian sense of the divine does not provide a natural perception appropriate to itself, all Christian experience must blend natural feeling, sentiment, and insight with what is believed in faith. The natural experiences are given a tone and an illumination by what is appreciated as necessarily absent to the wayfarer. Even the apostles needed faith in their experience of Christ. In writing about St. Thomas the Apostle and his encounter with the risen Christ, Gregory the Great says, "He saw one thing, he believed another. The divinity could not have been seen by a mortal man. So he saw a man but acknowledged God by saying, 'My Lord and my God.' By seeing he believed, and in recognizing the true man he cried out that he was God, the God he could not see."[2] All the natural experiences, with the various presentations they involve, are read and appreciated and felt in the light of what has to be absent, and, moreover, not in the light of just any sort of absence, but only of this singular kind which is appropriate to the God who could be all that he is, in undiminished goodness and greatness, even if there had been no world. This absence is not like that of things in the world, and the light it sheds is not like that of anything else.

But have we not overemphasized absence and the nonexperienced? Have we not drained the Christian sense of God of its affective importance in human life? Certainly there are the gifts of the Holy Spirit, Christian joy and delectation in God, the consolations of prayer, the sense mystics have of the Christian God, the Christian comfort that can come to those who are suffering, and the strength that fills martyrs. Are not such things experienced by believers? And is not God somehow present in them? Such things are experienced, but the experience of them is precisely the involvement of human feelings, sentiments, and insight in the act of faith, in the appreciation of the God who created and redeemed us. He is presented to us and addressed by us as the one who is absent in the way only he can be absent; as the one who therefore affects us in the way only he can affect us. In Christianity both God and the being of the world become mysteries and objects of contemplation in a way that does not occur in other religions. It may be this that Louis Bouyer has in mind when he writes that "mysticism properly so called is a purely Christian experience" and "the very notion of mysticism is one which appeared only in Christianity."[3] The categoriality of the Christian faith, its kerygma and statement, can indeed settle into the less articulated state of "religious experience" or "simple contemplation," but it never completely lets go. It must remain sufficiently there for us to be referred to God, in some minimal degree at least, and not simply to be lost in him. To be lost in him is the privilege of the beatific vision, not of our present state; we are always in need of someone to indicate God to us. Thus even St. John of the Cross, who claims that in true mystical experience "it is God himself who is perceived and tasted,"[4] says that the access we have to God in faith is more reliable than that given in religious perception: "It behoves [the soul] to keep the faith, even though the truths already revealed to it be revealed again; and to believe them, not because they are now revealed anew, but because they have already been sufficiently revealed to the Church; rather it must close its understanding to them, holding simply to the doctrine of the Church and to its faith, which, as Saint Paul says, enters through hearing."[5]

To live the Christian distinction between God and the world is not merely to grasp a theoretical distinction. It is not just the achievement of categoriality. It is more like living the distinction between husband and wife or child and parent. It engages our affections and takes place in our actions. It permits us to define ourselves in a way that could not occur without this distinction. It orders our dispositions and sentiments, including our religious sensibility, in a way in which it alone can order them. The world and the sacred have a Christian tone for us because of the Christian distinction in whose light we experience them, and the tone can become more pronounced for those who live the Christian life with greater dedication and love. But such experiencing insists precisely on a unique absence, on a term that must prompt faith and hope but not direct vision: "*Intra me et circa me es, et non te sentio*; you are within me and around me, and I feel you not" (*Proslogion*, ch. 17).[6]

NOTES

1. St. Hilary of Poitiers, *Tractatus super psalmos*, edited by Anthony Zingerle *Corpus scriptorum ecclesiasticorum latinorum*, vol. 22. (Vienna: Tempsky, 1891), p. 629; *Tractatus in psalmum CXXVII*, §§1 – 2.

2. St. Gregory the Great, *Homilia XXVI in Evangelia*, §8, in Migne, *Patrologia Latina*, vol. 76, col. 1202.

3. Louis Bouyer, *Introduction to Spirituality*, translated by Mary Perkins Ryan (Collegeville: Liturgical Press, 1961), p. 301.

4. St. John of the Cross, *Ascent of Mount Carmel*, II, XXVI, §5, from

The Complete Works of Saint John of the Cross, vol. 1, translated by E. Allison Peers (London: Burns, Oates and Washbourne, 1934).

5. Ibid., II, XXVII, §4.

6. On the relationship between Christian belief and political life see Appendix III, "Revelation and Political Philosophy."

12. Sacramental Life

Human action takes place within the whole which we call the world. Human action presupposes that the one who acts enjoys an understanding of his situation in the world and that he is able to imagine the situation as being different than it is. To execute an action is to change one's situation; if the change does not occur, the action has not taken place. The understanding we have of our situation and of the world as a whole comes initially from the community in which we live. We may passively assimilate the opinions of our community, or we may acquire more initiative, more mind, and begin to think for ourselves about our situation, about its possibilities, and about the whole. Even when we begin to think on our own, we do so from out of the setting our community provides. Philosophy is more than simply the attempt to determine our opinions about things in the world in which we live; it is the sustained and ordered attempt to see opinions as opinions, to see the world as the whole (to ask what it is to be the world or to be the whole). It is not just the attempt to think about our situation, but the attempt to consider the situation as situation, to think of ourselves as agents and as holders of opinions, to think of the opined as opined, the known as known.

When the Christian religious setting is introduced, the sense of the whole within which action takes place is profoundly changed. It is not simply that the whole is seen from a hitherto unrealized perspective within itself or that unnoticed features of the whole come into view. The whole itself is now "denied" — in a unique sense of denial — as being what is terminal. Still, this denial does not deprive the world of its

144

being the whole for reason and for human action. Furthermore, it is not that the world is now nested within another world or that the whole becomes a part of another whole similar to the first. The world or the whole is appreciated as that which might not have been, but it is so appreciated, and can be so appreciated, only in "contrast" to the God who would be all that he is if the world were not.

What is one to think and to do in the setting established by Christian belief? The necessities we must recognize are no longer just those that emerge as our mind is exercised in the world, and the natural, worldly necessities are no longer the final support for action. What we are to assert and what we are to do is shown in the actions and words of Christ, but the actions of Christ are not simply achievements carried on within the borders and necessities of the world. They were the first and fundamental questioning of the world, the introduction of the context in which God is most fully appreciated in contrast with the whole. The pattern for our behavior in this new setting is given to us in the multitude of events, parables, and maxims contained in the New Testament, and in the Old Testament as it is seen through the perspective of the New. The pattern is filled out by the actions of men and women who, in the history of the church, live in the imitation of Christ. But we understand that the substance of human actions in the imitation of Christ is not simply our human achievement; it is not defined by the borders and necessities that reason discloses, whether obscurely or clearly, in the world. We are now to imitate the generosity of God the creator and redeemer, and we are to estimate ourselves and others as created, redeemed, and loved by God. What we must now do requires something other than human agency. If our actions are to involve us in the life of God, the God who could be even if the world were not, then God must qualify what we do. The name given to this qualification of our activity is grace; it makes our actions like the actions of Christ and renders them fruitful in living in friendship with God. The dispositions that enable us to act in this graced way are the theological virtues of faith, hope, and charity, and what Aquinas has called the infused moral virtues.

But besides the moral actions performed in Christian life,

there are actions or events of a different kind that are called sacraments. What occurs in a sacrament can be understood only in the context in which the world is seen as created and as distinguished from the Christian God. If this setting is not appreciated, the sacraments become simply commemorations of a past event, signs of a community's decisions, expressions of someone's dispositions, or symbols of principles or truths. The theology of the sacraments must be placed not only within the context set by the incarnation but also explicitly within the context of creation as it is understood in Christian teaching. Without this setting the paradoxical formulations that are required to describe the sacraments become not mysteries but incoherences. Only in the setting of creation, with the transformation of language that it permits, can the identifications and distinctions that are required for sacramental theology be made.

Sacramental theology has distinguished two dimensions in each sacrament, a set of words (often called the "form" of the sacrament) and a material element (often called the "matter"). For example, the matter of the Eucharist is bread and wine, in baptism it is water, in confirmation it is holy oils, and in sacred orders it is the imposition of hands. It might be more precise, however, to add that the matter in a sacrament is, not simply the material thing, but the material thing taken or used in a certain way: not just the holy oils, but the oils used in anointing; not just water, but the water poured; not just bread and wine, but the bread and wine taken up and consumed. The sacrament involves not merely a material thing but a material thing involved in a gesture. In this way the sacraments reflect the incarnation, in which the Logos was not simply united with a body but entered into the life of a corporeal being. And with the material thing and gesture there is fused the formula, the words, that determine the sacrament. Both the words and the material in action are needed. The words alone are too intellectual to make up the concrete reality of the sacrament, and the material thing, even when it is involved in a gesture, is too undetermined.

But when the words are pronounced and the material element used, what is accomplished? A sacrament is a sign: its being is not exhausted in its physical performance and words. It brings forward something beyond its own words and material. The Eucharist, for example, is not simply bread and wine taken and consumed; it also signifies another nourishment. Baptism is not simply washing; it signifies another sort of cleansing and change. Moreover, the sacraments not only signify these other things but also bring them about. The sacraments effect what they symbolize. They symbolize and accomplish an action in our relationship with God. The sacraments are events in the life that we have by grace and that Christ has by nature, the life as sons of God the Father. They are episodes in that life, and in their material presence they also serve as signs to us of what occurs in them. But these occurrences can be properly formulated only with the transformation of language that happens when we begin to speak about God as creator of the world. Without the space provided by the Christian distinction the sacraments remain simply ceremonials, commemorations, or symbols. A sacrament can occur only when there is a need for actions and events in regard to the God who is not part of the world.

Furthermore, our engagement in the sacraments is a way of keeping the Christian distinction between God and the world alive for us; taking part in the sacraments restrains us from either reverencing the god of the philosophers or idolatrously worshipping the powers of the world. The sacraments are continuous lessons in the transcendence of God. Just as the incarnation brought out the full sense of God as creator, as the God who could become incarnate without destroying the integrity of what is by nature, so the sacraments make it clear that the God who can be present in the Eucharist, as we believe him to be present there, could not be a part of the world, nor could he be contained in the form of an idol. It is not that we just choose not to understand divinity in such ways or that we are simply commanded not to do so; rather the Christian sense of the divine does not lend itself to such interpretation, but it does allow us to think of God in a sacramental presence. The refinements necessary to allow us to receive the sacraments and to appreciate them as sacraments help keep Christian belief pure.

The being of sacraments as signs involves a complex pattern of relationships. The sacrament is first a sign of events accomplished by Christ when he lived among men. This is especially vivid in the Eucharist, which represents Christ's death on the cross. But the death of Jesus was more than the death of a human being; it was also the perfect sacrifice made by the Son to the Father. Because of this aspect the death of Christ redeemed mankind from sin. Now the Eucharist, being a sign and presentation of Christ's death, is also a sign of the divine achievement in the death of Christ. The Eucharist is not simply a sign of something else that happened in the world; it is a sign of something occurring in a context that goes beyond the mundane. In fact, only because the Eucharist is a presentation of our redemption before God can it also be an effective presentation of the death of Christ in world history. If the Eucharist did not present again our redemption before God, it would simply commemorate the death of Christ and not present it again.[1] In addition, the Eucharist is a sign of what it accomplishes for those who partake of it at the moment of its occurrence; it brings Christians into deeper union with Christ and with one another, and it intensifies their life with God by "nourishing" them. Finally, the Eucharist is a sign of the eternal life that it leads us toward: *et futurae gloriae nobis pignus datur*.

In this pattern of presences and representations the God present in the Eucharist is the same God who created the world, who could exist in undiminished goodness and greatness even if there were no world, who redeemed us in a generosity exceeding that of creation, the God with whom we hope to live eternally. The sacramental presence signifies beyond itself to the condition in which no representation will be required. Then the sacrament will give way to vision, and the union which is now always threatened by separation will yield to one that nothing can ever destroy. Just as "the visible presence of our Redeemer passed over into sacraments . . . and vision gave way to doctrine," so the sacraments in turn will pass over into a presence in which neither the divinity nor the humanity will lie hidden.[2] And the pattern of presentations in the Eucharist prompts us to pray appropriately in response: in adoration of what is present, in gratitude for what has been achieved, in petition for fidelity and in sorrow for failure, in hope for consummation.

These presentations are not to be understood as separate causes. It is not as though the sacrament first brings about the presence of the historical event, which in turn engages the divine transcendence, which in turn brings about our redemption and the promise of eternal life. Rather, all these dimensions are present at once in the sacrament and must be understood together. The formal structure of repeating the past, acting before God the Father, and anticipating future glory marks the way things occur in the life we are graced with as children of God. We live in the repetition of the life of Christ and in the hope that Christ will come again. The sacraments are not just external aids to this life. They establish its dimensions and make possible other nonsacramental actions in it, like prayer, penance, and charity. They provide the frame and exemplify the relationships of our life with God.

Moreover, the sacraments achieve this because they reflect the being of the incarnation. Christ did not just bring a teaching. He also did things, and his actions involved his bodily as well as his spiritual being. Christ as God incarnate was there to be responded to; he was there to have an effect on others. Similarly, the recipient of the sacrament responds to what occurs in it. The sacrament does not merely occasion the believer's response to God; it affects and changes him. The sacraments, and especially the Eucharist, emphasize the materiality of the incarnation. We respond, not just to a doctrine or to a sign, but to the presence of the divine in the mundane: a presence of the divine united with the human in Christ, and a continued presence of this union under the appearances of bread and wine.

The material element in the sacraments is not merely the material thing but the thing taken up into an action. The sacraments are an occurrence, not only an object. As occurrences they require someone who accomplishes them, the "minister" of the sacraments, and they require someone who is affected by them, the "recipient." How is the recipient of the sacraments to understand himself and what he does? Who is the "I" that is engaged in the sacraments? In our worldly activities we become identified, for ourselves and for others, as we differentiate ourselves from other persons and things. As we gradually begin to do things on our own, instead of being assimilated into the behavior of others, we appreciate that it is I who helped this person or insulted that one, who was cowardly in that situation or temperate in this. I become identifiable as the one who did this or that, and I become endowed with my character and my story, both of which, once achieved, are never separable from me. This character and story are displayed not only to me but to others, who can subsequently identify me to still others. My character, story, and reputation are built upon many strands in me that are assimilations from others. But I am not only what was assimilated; I have also begun certain actions that are more my own, for better or worse, than what I became before my own initiatives took place.

But in order to become myself in my actions, in order to be and to have a character, story, and reputation, I must also identify myself in a more rudimentary and more formal way. I must distinguish myself into the assimilator of what others say and the speaker of how things seem to me. I must be differentiated into myself as imagining and myself as imagined, into myself remembering and myself remembered, myself expecting and myself expected, into myself perceiving from here and myself perceived from there. These and other differentiations are needed for the self to be made actual: the "I" is that which is the same in all such distinctions. The formal differentiations and identities do not differ from one person to another in the way our characters, stories, and reputations differ. The formal patterns must be there if we are to be agents at all; they do not determine what kind of moral agent we have become.

The identifications and differences that establish us as selves are part of the natural necessities that occur within the whole that we call the world. They are patterns that not only establish the self but also help establish the world as the whole. The world is appreciated as the whole only by a privileged part of the world, by the dative of manifestation to whom the world is presenced. The world is the most diffuse and undifferentiated "this" ("all this") for one who can also say "I," one whose present is always the privileged "here" and "now." The self in the world appreciates, whether obscurely or clearly, whether mythically or conceptually, some of the necessities that must be in the world and for the self.

When in Christian faith the world is appreciated as that which, in contrast to the creator, might not have been, the believer's appreciation of himself as the dative for the world and for things in it is also affected. In place of the terminal opaqueness of one's self as simply being there — in the family, society, place and time in which one lives — there is the sense of being known and loved in a kind of unimaginable transparency, a clarity that makes our reputation, the solid and heavy opinions that others have of us, seem as nothing: "For how little it was that my tongue uttered of it in the ears even of my closest friends! Could they hear the tumult of my soul, for whose utterance no time or voice of mine would have been sufficient? Yet into your hearing came all that I cried forth in the anguish of my heart, and my desire was in your sight" (*Confessions*, VII 7).[3] Even the awareness we have of ourselves is dark compared to what God can see in us: "And even if I would not confess to you, what could be hidden in me, O Lord, from you to whose eyes the deepest depth of man's conscience lies bare? I should only be hiding you from myself, not myself from you" (X 2).

This understanding of himself as more visible to God than to himself or to anyone else is not simply an internal disposition Augustine adopts; it is related to how he must appreciate the world: "If one man merely sees the world, while another not only sees it but interrogates it, the world does not change its speech — that is, its outward appearance which speaks — in such a way as to appear differently to the two men; but presenting exactly the same face to each, it says nothing to the one, but gives answer to the other" (X 6). The world is appreciated as the creation of God: "We see the things you have

made, because they are; and they are, because you see them"
(XIII 38).[4] Augustine understands himself also as created, as
known and chosen by God, and in this understanding his life
becomes unsettled in a way that no worldly incident and no
philosophical reflection could provoke: "But do Thou, O my
God, hear me and look upon me and see me and pity me and
heal me, Thou in whose eyes I have become a question to
myself" (X 33).

Augustine's self-questioning and self-understanding arise, not
on the basis of a new perception, but within the understanding
of the world as created, which in turn is most fully appreciated
through belief in Christ as the Incarnate Son of God (VII
18− 21, X 43). But the Christian distinction between God and
the world works its way into our understanding and our behavior not only by virtue of prayer, reflection, and charity: it is
further disclosed and further confirmed by our engagement in
the sacraments. If there were no distinction between God and
the world, what we do in the sacraments would be nothing.
What occurs in the sacraments can take place only because
God is as we, in the Christian faith, believe him to be. The
activity of the sacraments is a constant reminder to us of who
God is and of what we are, a constant instruction about our
relationship with him. The sacraments are not only Christian
things but also Christian disclosures. And while the sacraments
make God present to us and modify our life with him, they
always do so in the form of signs, a form which is as much a
part of their being as is the presence they establish and the
effect they achieve. They exist for the wayfarer, who in receiv-
ing the sacraments must also be the one who obediently listens:
sed auditu solo tuto creditur.

NOTES

1. During the Reformation there was great controversy concerning
the Eucharist as a sacrifice. Catholics said that the Eucharist was an un-
bloody sacrifice and that the person celebrating the Mass functioned

as a priest: he offered sacrifice to God. However, the sacrifice was the same one as that offered in a bloody manner by Christ on the cross. Some Protestants claimed that there was only a single sacrifice, the one performed by Christ, and that the Eucharist commemorated it but did not enact a new sacrifice. This issue clearly revolves around the appropriate identification between the redemptive death of Christ and the Eucharist, and it might be clarified theologically by bringing out the special differences required for this identity to occur. The theoretical and historical issues in this controversy are clearly brought out by Francis Clark, S.J., *Eucharistic Sacrifice and the Reformation*, 2nd ed. (Oxford: Blackwell, 1967).

2. St. Leo the Great, *Sermo LXXIV, de Ascensione Domini II*, §3, in Migne, *Patrologia Latina*, vol. 54, col. 398.

3. St. Augustine, *Confessions*, translated by F.J. Sheed (New York: Sheed and Ward, 1944).

4. The theme of the createdness of the world provides the frame for the *Confessions* and is discussed in the last three chapters of the book.

Appendices

APPENDIX TO CHAPTER 6

Bibliographical and textual remarks concerning Aristotle's distinction between virtue and self-control. A good formulation of the issue of virtue and self-control can be found in Roger J. Sullivan, "The Kantian Critique of Aristotle's Moral Philosophy: An Appraisal," *The Review of Metaphysics* 28 (1974): 24–53. However, Sullivan does not exploit the distinction between virtue and continence in his recent commentary on Aristotle, *Morality and the Good Life* (Memphis: Memphis State University Press, 1977). Sullivan's essay was used extensively in a thesis written at the University of Toronto in 1979 by Paul R. Schwankl, *Kant's Treatment of Moral Character*. W.F.R. Hardie recognizes the difference between virtue and continence but is somewhat uncomfortable with it: "On the other hand, the merit of moral victory seems to be enhanced when there have been obstacles to overcome. Is the saint, or moral hero, the man who is not tempted or the man who struggles successfully with temptation?" *Aristotle's Ethical Theory* (Oxford: Oxford University Press, 1968), p. 138.

To comply more accurately with Aristotle's text, we must note that Aristotle also speaks of endurance as comparable to self-control, and softness or effeminacy as comparable to weakness in self-control (VII 1). He defines self-control (*enkrateia*) and weakness in self-control (*akrasia*) as ways of dealing with the pleasant, and endurance and softness as ways of dealing with the painful or the hard. Endurance is therefore a kind of forced, mastered analogue to courage, while softness is the helpless analogue to cowardice. These refinements are important and illuminating, but need not concern us any further; in our text we speak simply of self-control and weakness in self-control to refer to the kinds of character that fall between virtue and vice.

APPENDIX TO CHAPTER 9

A recent interpretation of St. Thomas' argument in *De ente et essentia* can be used to confirm the ideas we have developed from St. Anselm. See John Wippel, "Aquinas's Route to the Real Distinction: A Note on *De Ente et Essentia*," *The Thomist* 43 (1979): 279– 95. Wippel distinguishes two stages in Aquinas' argument. (1) Aquinas first establishes the point that there could not be more than one being in which essence and existence are the same; in all other beings essence and existence must be distinguished. Thomas shows this by canvassing the various ways multiplicity can occur and by showing that they could not apply to sheer existence. At this point, Wippel says, Aquinas has not proved that God exists, but he has shown that there could only be one God and that in all other beings essence and existence must be distinct: "The impossibility of there being more than one being in which essence and existence are identical is sufficient ground for [Aquinas] to conclude to their factual otherness in all else" (p. 295; the change in modality from the possible to the factual should be noted). (2) The next step of Aquinas' argument is to show that there cannot be only beings whose essence and existence are distinct. The fact that there are some such beings shows that there must also be a self-existing being (or else an infinite regress would occur). In this second step God's actual existence is shown.

What Aquinas does in stage (1) is parallel to what we, in our interpretation, have called introducing the Christian setting; it is parallel to what Anselm does when he introduces the Christian understanding of God and the world. Both God and all other

beings are understood in the setting of either existing or not
existing, and we understand that there could be only one being
whose essence is to exist. At this point we deal with a way of
understanding, which is covered by the question of what is
possible and what impossible. Within this way of being understood the beings and the world we encounter are seen not to be
existent through themselves. Their essence cannot be to exist.
Hence we conclude, in stage (2), to the actual existence of God.
But the question of the actual existence of God is preceded by
the issue of how God is to be understood, which is introduced
under the form that there could be only one being whose essence is to exist.

APPENDIX TO CHAPTER 11

Revelation and political philosophy. In discussing how Christian
experience differs from other kinds of human experience, it is
especially important to show how Christian belief is related to
the political life of human beings. The disaffiliation of religion
from the modern state has inclined recent political philosophers
to examine politics without paying much attention to religion,
and it has inclined theologians to pay scant attention to political
philosophy when they reflect on religious faith. Religion is
associated with morals, aesthetics, and personal self-
understanding, but its involvement in political life is neglected.
Such neglect is unfortunate and leaves the analysis of both religion and politics incomplete. In Greek and Roman philosophy,
in medieval Christian, Jewish, and Moslem thought, and even in
early modern thinking, when the state was being defined against
religion by writers like Machiavelli and Hobbes, the relationship
between religion and politics was expressly treated. An excep-
tion to the contemporary silence on religion and politics can be
found in the writings of Leo Strauss and the political philosophers who work under his influence. It will be convenient for
us to discuss the relationship between Christian faith and political life by commenting on some claims made in the Straussian
tradition.

It might appear that revealed religion introduces complications that make political life, or at least the political preservation of natural right, impossible. Walter Berns writes, "A revealed religion is revealed only to the godly, and the godly are only too likely 'to take advantage of the favor of revelation to demand political power for themselves or their allies'."[1] Revealed religion seems to imply that some members of the body politic are marked out as superior to others, not because of wealth or strength or virtue or intelligence or natural ability, but because they know and experience certain "ultimate truths" that others do not. The possession of these truths seems to justify them in ruling over the others. The truths in question may be unusual opinions about the natures of things, or they may be commands that, it is claimed, God issues to men above and beyond the obligations that are manifest in natural moral experience. Whether theoretical or practical, they are truths that are not available to people who have not been favored by revelation. They are available only to "the godly."

But this is not the kind of truth disclosed in revelation as it is understood by orthodox Christian faith. According to Christian belief there are no truths that are relevant for living the natural political life that are only available to those who adhere to Christianity. The truths dealing with political life and with virtue are available through the exercise of reason and choice. When one becomes a Christian, one is not apprised of yet other truths or divine commands that are politically relevant but not available to reason. Christian revelation leaves the natural necessities and natural truths intact, including all those that are at work in political life. The mysteries of Christianity, like the Trinity, grace, and redemption, are not new factors that undo the excellences and necessities of political life. Even belief in creation does not insert a relevant new factor into politics that is somehow concealed from those who do not believe. Christian belief does not establish a group of people who are supposed to govern others by virtue of the unusual opinions they possess.

It is difficult to isolate Strauss's own teaching on many issues because much of his writing consists of commentary on classical authors, and it is often not clear whether Strauss or the author being paraphrased is speaking. It seems, however, that by revealed religion Strauss means the communication of commandments whose necessity is not obvious to reason: "If what is required of man in relation to God is fidelity, trust, and obedience, then above all what is required is trust when all human assurance fails, obedience when all human insight fails."[2] The revealed commandments are not only not obvious to reason; they may even appear to be irrational. Strauss mentions Ibn Daud, for whom "the high example is the obedience of Abraham who made ready to sacrifice his son at the command of God, even though God had promised him that his son should be his heir, even though Abraham, had he wished to pretend to wisdom, could not but find that command absurd." But such an understanding of revealed religion is not the same as the Christian understanding of revelation. According to orthodox Christian thought what is good and obligatory by nature and according to reason remains such in Christian moral teaching, and remains as a kind of ballast for moral theology. The infused virtues may accentuate certain parts of natural morality, and they may bring out certain goods that are less clear to reason alone, but they do not work against the natural law.

It seems that the Straussian interpretation of revealed religion suffers from the failure to make an important distinction. In Straussian thought the distinction between nature and convention is made the pivot for political theory. In Christian belief the distinction between the natural and the supernatural is introduced. Perhaps it is inevitable that this Christian distinction should become dissolved in the Straussian interpretation into the distinction between nature and convention, with the supernatural — whether the mysteries of faith or the infused virtues and the obligations they involve — being interpreted as another form of the conventional. When this confusion occurs, the entire issue of Christian theology is simply not joined.

The interpretation of the supernatural as the conventional may also be related to Strauss's understanding of the biblical notion of God. He mentions "the central assumption of re-

vealed religion, namely, that God is unfathomable will."[3] In
discussing Maimonides he speaks of the biblical God "whose
essence is therefore indicated by 'Will,' rather than by 'Wisdom'."[4] But in Christian theology God is *primarily* not will *more*
than wisdom, nor is he will *rather* than wisdom; he is primarily
neither will nor wisdom but *esse subsistens*, on which both will
and wisdom are based. Besides emphasizing will so strongly,
Strauss at times seems to suggest that God can be considered
arbitrary or even tyrannical.[5] With this understanding of God
and divine power it is not surprising that Strauss sees Christian
moral teaching as conflicting with human excellence. He mentions "the Christian mistrust of purely human virtue, for the
sake of humiliating pride in its own virtues."[6] Such conclusions
follow if the special relationship between God and the world,
and between the divine and the natural, are not understood as
they are in orthodox Christian theology, with the integrity of
the natural preserved when it is taken in the new context of
creation and grace. And we may repeat what was said earlier,
that this understanding of the integrity of nature within grace
is, not the result of adding Greek philosophy to Christian religion, but the consequence of creation and the incarnation.

Among intellectuals there is currently little reverence left for
the gods of the city, although the Muses still find their wor-
shippers. Lionel Trilling remarks, "We are habituated to the
idea that society, though necessary for survival, corrupts the life
it fosters, and most of us give this idea some assent." There is
no good and no *kalon* to be admired in "society," the current
replacement for the city; there is only the compulsion of
necessity behind it. Yet Trilling is not without his divinities, for
he continues, "But we receive with no such tolerance the idea
that literature is an accomplice in the social betrayal. This of-
fends our deepest pieties."[7] Strauss is aware of the human
problem that arises when public and political life is deprived of
the sacred: "It is hardly necessary to add that the dogmatic
exclusion of religious awareness proper renders questionable all
long-range predictions concerning the future of societies."[8]
Strauss says that philosophy is always in tension with religious
belief, that Plato will always be in conflict with the poets and

Athens at odds with Jerusalem. Religion formulates for people, in a way that is persuasive to them, opinions about the ultimate, the sacred, the necessary, the obligatory, and the whole; philosophy criticizes such opinions, seeing them precisely as opinions. Philosophy can therefore be a destructive force if it dissolves the opinions by which men live, because most people will not be capable of comprehending necessities in their philosophical form; and having lost the security of their traditional opinions, they will not be able to keep any hold on what is necessary and obligatory. Philosophy is destructive when publicized, and the authorities know — or at least sense — this. They may persecute those who raise questions about the official opinions. Philosophical writing, therefore, has to be done in such a way as to communicate its substance to those who are able to appreciate it, while concealing its meaning from those who cannot, the "many" or the vulgar. Strauss observes that this sort of writing was quite generally practiced until the last two centuries and that we must keep this literary possibility in mind when we read texts and try to determine what they mean.[9]

As regards our present concerns, the question arises whether such principles of writing apply to Christian belief. Is Christian belief a set of opinions that are in tension with reason and the life of the mind? Strauss writes, "By becoming aware of the dignity of the mind, we realize the true ground of the dignity of man and therewith the goodness of the world, whether we understand it as created or as uncreated, which is the home of man because it is the home of the human mind."[10] Does such awareness call into question Christian belief and interpret it as convention and opinion? Is it necessary for a Christian writer only to pretend to be concerned with, say, creation and redemption, while actually being indifferent to them? Does a Christian writer have to choose between nature and creation and grace?

It would be instructive to know how Strauss interprets on this issue the writings of Thomas Aquinas; there seem to be indications in the Straussian oral tradition that Aquinas is considered to be more truly a philosopher than a believer. But the issue is not simply Aquinas as an individual; it is Aquinas as representing the thoughtful possibilities of Christianity. Aquinas does say that some truths about God ought not to be communicated to everyone because not everyone may be able to understand them; for example, the theological truth that God does not have feelings may disturb the faith of some people and may in some audiences be better left undiscussed. But this discretion is not the basic issue. What is basic is whether the truths of creation, redemption, the Trinity, grace, and eternal life are somehow to be deciphered by those who know; in regard to such teachings, are there different things to be said and held by the many on one hand and the the thinkers on the other? Or are we all "the same" in regard to the fundamental teachings of Christian faith, so that a nucleus of belief is needed by all? And can this element of belief be there without destroying the mind, with its dignity and excellence? Is this common belief compatible with the differentiation that occurs between those who exercise the mind and those who do not?

The Christian faith is such that it does not enter into competition with reason; its scope is other than the whole within which reason finds its home, but it leaves this home intact and reason intact within it. There is no need for a form of secret writing in these matters and no need for dissimulation of sense; not because believers just happen to be forthright people, but because the things believed do not necessitate a conflict between what is believed and what is known. The harmony that Christians expect between faith and reason was at the source of the establishment of the university as a peculiarly Christian institution. The rise of universities cannot be adequately explained by medieval European social and political conditions; it stems more profoundly from the way reason and faith are understood. This harmony was also at the root of the theological disputation, a public performance in which — in contrast to writing — one's position could not remain concealed, and in which objections had to be answered and not deflected. This harmony was behind Aquinas' impatient rebuke to the Latin Averroists: "But if there be anyone boasting of his knowledge, falsely so called, who wishes to say something against what we have written here, let him not speak in corners, nor in the presence of boys who do not know how to judge about such difficult matters; but let him write against this treatise if he dares."[11]

The harmony between faith and reason is achieved because of the special Christian understanding of God, who is not considered to be simply the best and greatest of all, but the God who could be all that he is, in undiminished goodness and greatness, even if the whole which we call the world, the place where the mind and reason are at home, did not exist. If, however, the divine is not understood as it is in Christian belief and theology, many of the paradoxes and contradictions that Strauss so well describes between religion and philosophy do in fact take place: if the divine is the best and highest being in the world, there will inevitably be tensions between the philosophical understanding of it and the opinions about it that support ordered public life.

NOTES

1. Walter Berns, *The First Amendment and the Future of American Democracy* (New York: Basic Books, 1976), p. 22. Berns quotes Harvey C. Mansfield, Jr. in this passage.

2. Leo Strauss, *Spinoza's Critique of Religion*, translated by E.M. Sinclair (New York: Schocken Books, 1965), p. 180.

3. Ibid., p. 212.

4. "How To Begin To Study *The Guide of the Perplexed*," in *Liberalism, Ancient and Modern* (New York: Basic Books, 1968), p. 177.

5. Ibid., p. 180; and see *Thoughts on Machiavelli* (Seattle: University of Washington Press, 1969), pp. 49 – 50, 118. This theme in Strauss is developed by Harvey C. Mansfield, Jr. in *Machiavelli's New Modes and Orders: A Study of the Discourses on Livy* (Ithaca: Cornell University Press, 1979).

6. *Spinoza's Critique of Religion*, p. 50; see *Thoughts on Machiavelli*, pp. 188 – 90.

7. Lionel Trilling, *Sincerity and Authenticity* (Cambridge: Harvard University Press, 1972), pp. 60 – 61.

8. "An Epilogue," in *Liberalism, Ancient and Modern*, p. 219.

9. See Strauss, *Persecution and the Art of Writing* (Glencoe: The Free Press, 1952), chapter 2.

10. "What Is Liberal Education?" in *Liberalism, Ancient and Modern*, p. 8. On the same page Strauss says, "We cannot exert our understanding without from time to time understanding something of importance; and this act of understanding may be accompanied by the understanding of understanding, by *noēsis noēseōs*, and this is so high, so pure, so noble an experience that Aristotle could ascribe it to his God."

11. St. Thomas Aquinas, *On the Unity of the Intellect against the Averroists*, §124, translated by Beatrice H. Zendler (Milwaukee: Marquette University Press, 1968), p. 75.

Index